Criminal Justice

Recent Scholarship

Edited by
Marilyn McShane and Frank P. Williams III

A Series from LFB Scholarly

Serious Crime and the Public Consumption of Alcohol

Ronald R. Thrasher

LFB Scholarly Publishing LLC
New York 2001

Library of Congress Cataloging-in-Publication Data

Thrasher, Ronald R.
Serious crime and the public consumption of alcohol / Ronald R. Thrasher.
p. cm. -- (Criminal justice)
Includes bibliographical references and index.
ISBN 1-931202-12-5 (alk. paper)
1. Alcoholism and crime--United States--Case studies. 2. Law enforcement--United States--Case studies. 3. Drinking of alcoholic beverages--United States--Case studies. 4. Drunkeness (Criminal law)--United States--Case studies. I. Title. II. Criminal justice (New York, N.Y.)
HV5056.U6 T47 2001
364.2'4--dc21

2001000673

ISBN 1-931202-12-5

Printed on acid-free 250-year-life paper.

Manufactured in the United States of America.

TABLE OF CONTENTS

1. INTRODUCTION 1

Research Focus 4
Setting 5
Context 6
Definition of Terms 7
Overview of the Work 12
Notes 14

2. THEORETICAL FRAMEWORK 15

Hirschi's Social Control 16
Reckless' Containment Theory 18
Beccaria's Deterrence Doctrine 20
Cognition 28
Notes 31

3. A MODEL OF SOCIAL CONTROL 33

Assumptions 33
Rationale 35
Predictions 37
Hypothesis 38
Notes 39

4. METHODOLOGY 41

Research Objective and Strategy 41
Ethnography 44
Survey 45
Non-Participant Observation 47
Bar Classifications 48
Ethical Considerations 48
Validity and Reliability 49
Study Strengths 51
Notes 53

5. DATA.. 55

Stillwater Ethnography.. 55
Street Parties.. 56
Crime Rate Data 62
Stillwater Hotel Bar.. 69
Stillwater Neighborhood Bar.. 74
Stillwater Restaurant Bar.. 77
Stillwater Theme Bar... 80
Ponca City Ethnography... 85
Ponca City Hotel Bar... 86
Ponca City Neighborhood Bar...................................... 89
Ponca City Restaurant Bar.. 93
Ponca City Theme Bar... 96
Summary.. 98
Notes..101

6. DATA ANALYSIS 105

Stillwater Crime Analysis..109
Chico Crime Analysis..113
Summary...117
Notes..118

7. CONCLUSION 119

REFERENCES CITED..123

APPENDIX A — Local Ordinances.......................................135

APPENDIX B — Crime Statistics and Analysis.....................157

INDEX...169

LIST OF TABLES

1. Rates of Death Caused by Alcohol, per 100,000 persons .. 2
2. Stillwater Sales Tax Amounts 61
3. Crime Rates Before, During, and After Drinking Ban 63
4. Stillwater Before and During Crime Rate
5. Analysis of Variance 65
6. Stillwater Before, During, and After Crime Rate
7. Analysis of Variance 65
8. Stillwater Crime Rates Post hoc Test.......................... 66
9. Crime Rates/Trends Before and After
10. Public Drinking Ban.. 68
11. Analysis of Variance Table.......................................106
12. Enforcement of Public Drinking Bans........................109
13. Number of Arrests During Stillwater s
14. First Public Drinking Prohibition 110
15. Number of Public Drinking Arrests,
16. Crime Rate Comparisons..111
17. Number of Warnings During Stillwater s
18. Second Public Drinking Prohibition..........................112
19. Number of Warnings, Crime Rate Comparisons..........113

LIST OF FIGURES

1. Beccaria s Deterrance Model 23
2. Conceptual Social Control Model of Criminal Behavior 34
3. Methods Summary 42
4. Stillwater Sales Tax 60

CHAPTER 1

Introduction

During 1993 U.S. police arrested almost three million persons under the age of 18. These arrests accounted for only 13 percent of known violent offenses (Maguire and Pastore, 1994). In 1996 youths ages 12 to 20 accounted for 9.5 million drinkers. Of these, 4.4 million practice binge drinking. The same study indicated that 45 percent of students grades six to eight reported drinking within the previous year (Bilchik, 1998). The US Department of Education (1993) reports that as many as 52 percent of college age offenders were under the influence of alcohol when they committed their crime. The National Criminal Justice Association (1998) calculates that alcohol is involved in 40 percent of violent crimes and fatal accidents. This equals over 183,000 rapes, 197,000 robberies, 661,000 aggravated assaults and 1.7 million simple assaults annually.

The common perception and the research literature support a strong positive correlation between alcohol consumption and crime (Stitt and Giacopassi, 1992). In a 1987 survey, the Department of Justice found that almost 32 percent of juveniles housed in long-term juvenile institutions were drunk while committing their offense. The survey also reported that over 55 percent of the juveniles admitted that they drank at least once a week the year before being arrested. Washbrook (1977) surveyed 5,000 Birmingham, England adult prisoners and found that 54 percent consumed alcohol within 24 hours before committing their criminal act.

The relationship between alcohol and crime persist both in public and in the home. Murdoch, Pihl and Ross (1990) found a positive correlation between domestic violence and either offender, victim, or offender and victim drinking. National surveys indicate that 27 percent of respondents say that alcohol causes family trouble (Maguire and Pastore, 1993). Temple (1998) reports that half of college students experiment with binge drinking. O Neal (1998) found that drinking has become such a problem among college students that 40 percent of four-year schools either allow drinking on campus or operate campus bars. These schools believe that by operating their own bar, colleges can better control binge, underage, and crime related drinking problems.

More recently, alcohol related problems appear to be lessening. Looking only at arrest, Chaiken and Robinson (1998) report that rates of arrest for driving under the influence of alcohol (DUI) have decreased by 24 percent since 1990. Considering behavior independent of arrest, they found that alcohol-related highway fatalities decreased by 29 percent since 1988.

The National Center for Health Statistics (1997) compile data on the alcohol-related deaths to victims treated at trauma centers. These incidences also indicate decreases.

Table 1
Rates of Death Caused by Alcohol Per 100,000 Persons

Year	All Groups	White Males	White Females	Black Males	Black Females
1980	8.4	10.8	3.5	32.4	10.6
1985	7.0	9.2	2.8	27.7	8.0
1990	7.2	9.9	2.8	26.6	7.7
1992	6.8	9.9	2.6	22.3	6.3
1993	6.7	9.7	2.7	21.3	5.5
1994	6.8	9.9	2.7	20.4	5.6
Average	7.15	9.9	2.85	25.12	7.28
Percent Change	-19.0%	-8.3%	-22.9%	-37.0	-47.2%

*Data Source: National Center for Health Statistics, Monthly Vital Statistics

What causes the relationship between alcohol consumption and crime? Is this relationship changing? Is this exclusively an American relationship? Homel, Thomsen and Thommeny (1992) found public factors including intoxication level, patron mix, comfort level, boredom, police presence, legislation, and bureaucratic controls contribute to violence. Homel, Tomsen and Thommeny concluded that, promotions which cause mass intoxication should be banned; but, responsible serving practices on their own may not greatly influence levels of violence.

Many of these studies and conclusions are problematic. Self-report surveys concerning domestic violence can be influenced by divorce, support payments, child custody and individual psychological repression. Police records may be no more reliable. Many court decisions prohibit the filing of a public intoxication charge for an offense that occurred in the privacy of an individual s home.[1] When filing charges for a serious crime, police may consider an additional public intoxication charge as stacking charges and not file the alcohol count.[2]

Many individuals and communities consider drunkenness and public consumption of beer as representative of nuisance laws similar to vagrancy, begging or some forms of street vending or performing. As such, communities and police do not universally apply and enforce these laws. The laws many times lack a well-defined victim. Even many public drinking laws do not prohibit drinking, only public drinking. And, although there appears to be a correlation between alcohol consumption and serious crime, no relationship between public drinking and serious crime has been established.

Police may also be hesitant to file an alcohol charge knowing that the charge requires mandatory sober-up jail time before release. This forces police administrators to balance the liability issues of jailing someone to sober-up, at night, without seeing a judge, against releasing an intoxicated person on bail who may become a threat to him/herself or others. Kansas for example, decriminalizes public intoxication by defining drunkenness as a disease rather than a crime. These issues distort available information and limit researching the relationship between alcohol and serious crime.

This project looks specifically at serious crime and a possible association with public beer drinking. If a significant decrease in serious crime is found when beer drinking is restricted to inside bars and taverns, then what differences are present when people drink inside bars opposed to drinking on public streets and sidewalks? What is the impact of aggressive verses laissez-faire enforcement? Identifying and understanding these concepts and social forces could lead to significant crime control strategies with minimal intrusions to personal liberties.

Research Focus

This project focuses on the relationship between public consumption of beer and adult serious crime. We know that issues surrounding alcohol consumption and serious crime constitute major social problems. We also know that alcohol and crime touch wide populations. Finally, the relationships between alcohol and crime permits generalizations to broad aspects of social theory. For these reasons, alcohol and crime represent timely social problems critically in need of explanation and pragmatic research.

Theoretically, this research builds on a model of social control and deterrence. The inductive methodology begins with a case study of my research on street party experiences. These experiences form a theoretical explanation of social controls that explain decreases in serious crimes when public beer drinking is restricted by local law. I expand and generalize traditional social control models by incorporating deterrence doctrine to explain previously unexplained phenomena. Deterrence doctrine provides the basic structure for my model and provides a mechanism for driving the model. Social control provides alternative forms and degrees of punishment. Cognition, imbedded in learning theory provides feedback that folds back upon itself to reinforce and tie together the deterrence and social control aspects of the model. Together these components build the research process.

Setting

This project began as a case study supported by the Stillwater, Oklahoma Police Department. The Department asked me to develop ways to control large, highly intoxicated crowds after sporting events and during annual street parties. I began this project with a review of local historical events.

Within the past 25 years, Stillwater, Oklahoma experienced two distinct annual street parties. The first party evolved from the streaking fad, which swept college campuses in the early 1970s.[3] This party flourished annually for five years then slowly died following enactment of a local ordinance prohibiting beer drinking on city streets and sidewalks. Four years following enactment of the public drinking prohibition, voters overturned the ordinance. The second annual street party resulted primarily from the marketing efforts of a local bar. This second party suddenly died the year after re-enacting a similar law, again prohibiting public beer drinking.

To understand these street party events I begin with a study of Stillwater, Oklahoma and the two street party experiences. Stillwater is also the setting of non-participant observation of drinking behavior inside and outside of bars and taverns. Because Stillwater enacted public beer drinking prohibitions, overturned the prohibition, then re-enacted a similar law, I also examined before, during, and after crime rates.

The study then moved to Ponca City, Oklahoma. Ponca City represents a similar community that allows public beer drinking. I conducted non-participant observation of various bars in Ponca City to provide a comparison to the Stillwater data.[4]

Finally I compiled a list of communities with similar public drinking prohibitions and repeated the statistical comparison of before and after crime rates. The cities selected include Ada, Oklahoma; Velma, Oklahoma; Manhattan, Kansas; Boulder, Colorado; Moore, Oklahoma; Durant, Oklahoma; Edmond, Oklahoma; Sapulpa, Oklahoma; Lawton, Oklahoma; Jenks, Oklahoma; Lawrence, Kansas; and Chico, California.

Context

Harper (1982) uses the term context to describe his personal background, experiences, and biases as an investigator. Following this tradition, this section provides some insight into my experiences with drinking, bars and individual behavior within these social settings.

I neither drank nor visited bars in high school. In 1971, I enrolled as an incoming freshman at Oklahoma State University. Even in my early college experiences, I seldom visited bars. My first experience with drinking followed my joining a new fraternity. In this environment, I watched the mind and behavior altering effects of alcohol.

During my fraternity experience, two members left college to become police officers. These contacts provided me with jobs working security at various construction sites and apartment complexes. Gradually I began working the higher-paying jobs as bouncer in bars and dance halls. Eventually, I started a business with one other person providing security for bars, banks and dance halls throughout central and western Oklahoma.

After six years, just short of an undergraduate degree, I tired of college and went to work as a police officer for the Stillwater, Oklahoma, Police Department. After a year on the police department, I found myself assigned to alcohol enforcement, patrolling many of the same bars that I previously worked. I worked alcohol enforcement for two years until, through promotions, I began to move up through the ranks of the police department.

For the last fifteen years I have commanded several units associated with bars and drinking. One unit investigates criminal activity, much of which is associated with alcohol. One unit oversees licensing and patrolling bars. Another unit performs the crime analysis of drinking related offenses. These traditionally include public intoxication (PI) and driving under the influence of alcohol (DUI). I also investigate internal affairs complaints against police officers. An off-duty police officer drinking in a bar seems to generate citizen complaints regardless of the officer s behavior. Finally, I performed research on proposed policies and ordinances that look for ways to decrease violent crime.

Clearly these experiences could bias my observations and results. However, I plan to use these experiences as references to compare, contrast and understand my social psychological observations. I will in this study make every effort to provide unbiased observations and interpretations of the data.

Definition of Terms

Several concepts and a number of terms require definition. The first concept concerns adult serious crime. I define adult serious crime as index crimes or Uniform Crime Report (UCR) Part I offenses. Sometimes called index crimes, Adler, Mueller and Laufer (1991) define Part I offenses as those crimes most serious in nature and most likely to become known to police if they occur. The Federal Bureau of Investigation (FBI) (US Department of Justice, 1984) began tracking crimes in the United States in the early 1930s. Within that tracking system, dimensions of index crimes became specified as: murder, rape, robbery, aggravated assault, burglary, larceny and auto theft.[5]

Advantages of the FBI system include a uniform, specific definition of each offense. This becomes particularly helpful when a larceny under California State law, for example, becomes a burglary if committed in Utah under Utah State law. Other advantages include the general acceptance of index crimes as an indicator of criminal activity, their long-time usage and widespread availability. Disadvantages of the index crime system become apparent with subjective comparisons. For example, a community with 20 shopliftings and no murders may be very different from a community with no shoplifting and 20 murders although they share the same crime rate. Likewise, a community with 20 individuals each committing a single murder may be very different from a community with a single serial offender. Crime rate then becomes the number of a particular type of crime (or the total number of index crimes) known to police for a given population over a given period of time.

The final concern with using UCR data is the National Incident Based Reporting System (NIBRS). In the late 1970s, the U.S. Department of Justice (DOJ), Federal Bureau of Investigation (FBI), with a grant from the Bureau of Justice Statistics (BJS), began an evaluation study of the UCR system of reporting crime in America. The study concluded that the UCR system does not permit the examination of complex relationships among characteristics of criminal events (National Criminal Justice Association, 1997). The study went on to recommend:

- revision of the definitions of certain Index offenses;
- identification of additional significant offenses to be reported;
- refining definitions for both;
- development of data elements (incident details) for all UCR offenses in order to fulfill the requirements of incident-based reporting versus the current summary reporting.

In 1985, the FBI and the BJS implemented the NIBRS reporting program on an experimental basis. NIBRS reports individual characteristics about criminal offenders and their individual offenses. UCR only reports the most serious offense in a continued criminal enterprise. For example, an offender who commits a kidnapping, rape, and murder would only be reported as one murder under the UCR system. Under NIBRS, the kidnapping, the rape and the murder would each be counted as separate crimes under a single incident. Additionally NIBRS Group A offenses include 22 crimes compared to seven UCR Part I offenses. Definitions of individual offenses under NIBRS also differ slightly to the same offense defined by UCR.

Today contribution to NIBRS rather than UCR remains voluntary on the part of law enforcement agencies throughout the United States. Many agencies still contribute to UCR because of the cost of computer upgrades, new software and new report forms. For these reasons, I only considered crime data submitted on the UCR format and criteria.

The second concept involves public drinking. Many parts of the United States, particularly in the South and the Midwest, prohibit public consumption of liquor or hard spirits (Black, 1979). This study concerns a more recent phenomena, the prohibition of drinking beer in public. Since beer generally contains less alcohol, beer traditionally faces different tax structures and drinking restrictions than liquor. Only in the last 30 years have a number of communities begun experimenting with laws against public consumption of beer. For example, in Oklahoma the public consumption of liquor is prohibited statewide.[6] Local ordinance regulates public beer drinking.

Public drinking in this study involves drinking on public streets, alleys, sidewalks and areas of public property (parks, picnic areas, sporting complex and other public areas). Areas such as bars, taverns, restaurants, private property and private parking lots fall outside the definition of public drinking for this project. Observations of drinking behavior around a bar, for example, on private property follow within the legal definition of a curtilage. Black (1986) generally defines a curtilage as a courtyard of space or ground adjoining a house (or business) necessary and convenient and habitually used for purposes of the family (or business).

The third concept of perceived social control comes from the theoretical tradition. From a criminological perspective, social controls are those social forces that influence individuals to conform to social norms. In this project, I classify perceived social control both by social settings and source.

Social settings include inside a drinking establishment, outside a drinking establishment (i.e. a parking lot or curtilage), public streets, sidewalks, alleys and other public areas. Sources of perceived social control include: strangers; acquaintances; and authority figures. Further dimensions include degrees of interaction such as awareness, personal contact and the threat of formal sanction such as being thrown out of a bar or being arrested. Definitions of social control with its various dimensions become clearer following a discussion of the theoretical tradition of social control.

I established four general categories to define the term bar.[7] These include the theme bar, the restaurant bar, the hotel/motel bar and the neighborhood bar. Although themes and clientele often overlap, a predominate category usually appears.

Theme bars include a wide variety of bars that cater to a particular subject. Examples include sports bars, gay bars, college bars, ethnic bars, strip bars, singles bars, and others. These bars become easily identifiable by their decor, atmosphere and clientele. Singles bars usually lack the sports paraphernalia that cover the walls and surround the big-screen televisions of the typical sports bar. Sports bars lack the characteristic raised stage and brass dance pole almost always present in a strip bar. Likewise, a young female seeking male companionship would likely feel out-of-place in a gay bar just as a gay man might feel out of place in a biker bar. Even though the themes may differ, the social force that defines each of these bars becomes some type of predominate theme.

Food represents the primary focus of the restaurant bar. In this bar, drinking accentuates and supports eating. There may be a decorating theme incorporated into the food and furnishings, but the focus is food. People come to eat and may drink before, during, or after their meal. People do not come to the restaurant bar to associate with people with similar interest and backgrounds. A person soon begins to feel uncomfortable sitting in a restaurant bar only to watch the football game with other football fans. On the other hand, a gay person eating at one table might feel very comfortable with someone at the next table who typically frequents bisexual singles bars. Food becomes the attachment to the restaurant bar. If the food or service is bad, the patron is not likely to return.

The hotel bar caters to lodging. There may also be a theme in the hotel bar, but this theme is often regionally based. For example, a hotel near an amusement theme park or nearby historical monument might carry the theme of the local attraction. Themes also frequently change in hotel bars. The basketball theme when the local college hosted the play-offs may change to an elephant theme for a Republican fund-raiser. Like the restaurant bar, the hotel bar is likely to attract a wide range of patrons. The elderly couple lodging in the hotel on vacation might complain if the Elks convention becomes too loud, but it would not cause them to feel uncomfortable and out-of-place. In the hotel bar the lonely traveler may feel at home for a considerable time while looking for companionship or waiting for a meeting. Lodgers attachment to the hotel bar is lodging, business or some event at the hotel such as a seminar or convention. Patrons do not return to the hotel bar without the reoccurrence of a particular convention, business or lodging need.

The final category is the neighborhood bar. This is more than a bar for people who frequent a geographic area. A theme may be present. But, it may be well out of date and never changed. It may also be a theme that nobody notices. The bar itself is likely to be something of an institution within the community or subculture. This is the bar where everyone knows everyone and everyone feels at home. Patrons provide assistance and may attend the funeral of other patrons. A newcomer would be keenly aware of this atmosphere and may even be questioned by the regulars. A right of passage precedes feeling at home in the neighborhood bar. For many, this substitutes as a therapeutic environment, a place to escape, a place to tell someone your problems. Cheers, from the popular television situation comedy provides an excellent example of the neighborhood bar. Patrons of the neighborhood bar are not likely to visit other bars. In this sense customers remain static over time and loyal to the bar.

I define punishment as any negative anxiety-producing event ranging from embarrassment to death. Fear in the form of anxiety becomes a negative stimulus for behavior generating from formal or informal cognition. Finally, cognition is learning, processing and decision making processes performed at various levels of consciousness generally from observation, experience, conditioned behavior, social forces, inductive or deductive reasoning.

Cognition includes both rationally choosing between options and normative behavior. Normative behavior describes that activity, generally on the preconscious level, where a generalized stimulus evokes a socialized, normative or conditioned response.

Overview of the Work

Chapter 1 examines the social impact of alcohol consumption and the project s historical background and setting. It defines additional terms and concepts used in the study.

Chapter 2 reviews the major contributors to social control theory. It specifically pays attention to deterrence doctrine. I examine deterrence based upon its historical significance, its lack of modern academic support and its understated public following in the form of stiffer penalties for crime and the assumed need for more police and prisons.

Chapter 3 integrates these social control theories into a testable model of social control. The chapter contains conceptual assumptions, statements of dependent and independent variables, mechanisms, predictions and rationales. The chapter concludes with the project hypothesis.

Chapter 4 describes the various methodologies used to conduct the study. It begins with a case study of two street parties that serves as the catalyst for one community s public beer drinking prohibitions. The methodology also includes non-participant observation of drinking behavior in and around various types of bars. This observation includes similar type bars in communities who allow public beer drinking and in communities where public drinking is prohibited. Finally, I survey a number of communities who prohibit public beer drinking and statistically compare crime rates before and after enacting public drinking prohibitions.

Chapter 5 presents data and results obtained by the study. It includes a detailed description (Geertz, 1973) of both the street party case studies and the non-participant observation conducted in various type bars. The chapter also identifies communities with public drinking prohibitions and compares communities before and after crime rates.

Chapter 6 analyzes the data from the perspective of the research hypothesis and the data collected. It compares and contrasts those communities with the most significant decrease in serious crime after enacting public drinking prohibitions. It also further examines those communities with less significant impact from their public drinking prohibitions.

Chapter 7 presents the conclusion. It analyzes the data within the perspective of the theoretical model and presents both an explanation and an application for the apparent success of many modern community-policing theories and programs.

NOTES

[1] See Oklahoma State Statutes, Title 37, Chapter 8 Consuming or Inhaling Intoxicants in Public Places; *(Drink) (inhale intoxicants) (drink intoxicants) in (public) (prohibited) place.*

[2] Stacking charges refers to the filing of multiple criminal charges on the same or included behavior or action. An example would be when an intoxicated person steals an item. Some prosecutors would consider filing both a larceny charge and a public intoxication charge stacking charges.

[3] Streaking was a fad consisting of people running naked through public areas. Associated with flashing (wearing nothing except a long coat and periodically opening the coat to public view), the fad was nation wide and affected popular music and even the Academy Awards was once streaked. Both streaking and flashing were associated with this event.

[4] By non-participant observation, I mean that I will not be consuming alcoholic beverages while collecting data for this project.

[5] Arson was later added as an index crime. Because arson data is not historically available, arson statistics are excluded in this study.

[6] See Oklahoma State Statutes, Title 37, Section 537 {A} 8.

[7] Throughout this project I use the terms bar and tavern synonymously.

CHAPTER 2

Theoretical Framework

The study of individual behavior within group settings defines sociology. Defining socialization becomes more problematic. Mead (1934), a symbolic interactionalist, describes socialization as ...when a generalized other internalizes so that the community exercises control over the conduct of it s individuals... Berger and Luckmann (1966), phenomenologists, describe socialization as the internalization of societal values and norms. Campbell (1975) while discussing dual inheritance theory addresses socialization as ...(the) universal tendency for conformity to the opinion of others.... Parsons and Bales (1955), structural functionalists, defines socialization as a shared symbolic system which functions in interaction....

Each of these definitions shares the underlying assumption that individuals become socialized by their contact with others.[1] Williams and McShane (1994) tie this interaction to social control theory by saying, Another way to look at social control theory is to call it socialization theory. Since un-socialized humans, babies, for example, will simply act out their desires, it is the presence of other people that necessitates that those behaviors be controlled. Social control assumes that individuals have the capacity and possibly the desire for deviant behavior. Social control theorists ask what causes conformity. Social control theory provides one explanation.

Modern social control theory began with the work of Thomas Hobbes. Hobbes wrote that people possessed a basic evil instinct.[2] Later, Durkheim (1895) theorized that deviance becomes a normal aspect of any society. Even a society of saints experiences some type of deviate behavior. Durkheim believed society controls deviance by expressions of displeasure or punishment. In this way, deviance acts as a boundary maintenance device. Anomie results with the breakdown of boundary controlling devices or other mechanisms of social control. It is this breakdown that causes increases in deviance.

The most cited social control theories include: Travis Hirschi s social bonding, Walter Reckless containment, and Cesar Beccaria s deterrence theory. Each accepts deviant behavior as natural. Hirschi (1969) suggests that attachment, commitment, involvement, and belief systems contribute to social bonds that control this natural deviant behavior. Reckless (1973) describes inner and outer containment against pushes and pulls as an explanation of social control. Becarria (1764) suggests that the certainty, celerity, and severity of punishment deter crime.

Hirschi s Social Control

Hirschi (1969) suggests attachment, commitment, involvement and belief systems contribute to social bonds that "control" natural deviate behavior. In this way, social bonds describe and categorize the socialization process. These bonds function both independently and collectively to prevent deviate behavior.

Attachment describes the bond to individuals and institutions. The degree of attachment is how much one cares about other people and organizations. Hirschi (1969) believes attachment bonds contribute the most to social control. Examples of individual bonds include relatives, teachers and friends. Institutional bonds include church, school and athletic organizations. Hirschi describes attachment bonds as superego control and the lack of attachment bonds as a cause of psychopathic development.

Commitment bonds develop as time and efforts are devoted to things such as job advancement, educational achievement and reputation development. Commitment includes the idealized pursuit as well as the actual investment. For example, if an individual spends two years toward a college degree or works for a job promotion, s/he risks this investment by criminal behavior. From this perspective, commitment becomes rational choice. Hirschi (1969) asks, Do I want to risk ten years in prison and all those years getting an education over a ten dollar robbery?

Involvement bonds occur when an individual s time is filled with non-deviate activities. Many persons undoubtedly owe a life of virtue to a lack of opportunity to do otherwise (Hirschi, 1969). For example, youths who spend much of their time with family, school or a youth group, do not have time for deviance.

Belief systems develop as people accept moral validation of social norms. Belief systems require individuals to first accept social norms as reasonable and fair. People then internalize those norms where a violation becomes a moral wrong. This assumes a common value system and that people internalize social norms differently. Ultimately, belief systems become a matter of degree. The stronger the belief in the social norm, the stronger the social bond becomes, and the less likely the development of criminal behavior.

Hirschi (1969) tested his theory by self-report questionnaires. He surveyed 4,077 California junior and senior high school students. The survey tested both the strengths of social bonds and measured delinquency on the part of the students. Results indicate a negative correlation between increasing strength of social bonds and increasing amounts of delinquency. Hirschi interpreted these results as support for his social control theory.

Others replicating this research also used self-report surveys involving thousands of school age youth. Generally, researchers found significant positive correlations between social bonds and delinquency. However, different researchers found different bonds more highly correlated and some researchers found relationships with bonds other than those developed by Hirschi (1969).

Critics attack the methodological problems associated with self-report surveys administered only to youths. Also, the relationship between various social bonds and the strength of individual bonds is not well developed. Finally, does weakening of the social bonds cause delinquency, or does delinquency cause the weakening of the social bonds? Overall, evidence of social bonds exists. The theory is not, however, as widely accepted as it was when originally proposed.[3]

Reckless Containment Theory

Walter Reckless (1973) containment theory provides a straightforward approach to conforming behavior. First, Reckless describes forces that push (or pull) a person into deviant behavior. Reckless then describes control systems that counter these deviant forces. Systems act either psychologically from inside the individual or socially from outside. The stronger or more developed system determines conformity or deviance. Sandhu (1977) writes that Reckless explains social control from both psychological/sociological and macro/micro perspectives. Reckless described his theory as more middle-range and not descriptive of every type of criminal behavior. Reckless further limits his theory to explaining conformity and deviance, but not pathology arising from neuroses, psychoses, obsessions/compulsions, or organic brain disorders.

The first and most important protection from deviance is inner containment. This represents a personal internalization of social norms. It originates from a psychoanalytic perspective and varies between individuals. Similar to ego-development, inner containment consists of personal forces like individual identity, responsibility, conscience, self-control and tolerance. Inner containment forms during youth and most often represents a good (or bad) self-concept. Reckless (1973) argues that the more developed an individual s image of him/herself, the more resistant the individual becomes to deviant behavior.

Outer containment consists of social forces outside the individual. Examples include the legal system, expected roles, social norms, religious or school groups and provisions for alternative behavior.[4] These forces become much more sociological and provide another explanation for conforming or deviate behavior.

Push factors operate from within and work against containment. Pushes consist of any variety or combination of stresses, anxieties, frustrations, rejections and alienation s. More specific examples include anger, hostility, disappointments and inferiority feelings. The balance of inner containment and pushes provide one explanation for conforming/deviate behavior on the individual level.

Pull factors originate from the social environment as external factors. These also work against containment. Pulls include criminal or delinquent subcultures, gangs, unemployment, poverty, minority membership and blocked opportunities for success. The balance between outer containment and pulls provides the final mechanism for conforming/deviate behavior.

Reckless and Dinitz (1972) tested their theory by interviewing teachers in inner city Columbus, Ohio neighborhoods. Teachers selected 125 boys whom the teachers identified as good boys. These boys lacked a criminal record, interacted well with teachers and parents, had good self-esteem, scored high on social responsibility test and scored low on delinquency proneness test. Later Reckless and Dintz interviewed teachers, parents and boys identified as bad boys. Both groups of boys took the same battery of self-esteem tests. With this comparison, Reckless concluded that boys with a good self-image (even though they came from a bad social environment) were less likely to become involved in criminal activity.

Containment theory also draws criticism. Labeling theorists question the effects of labeling good and bad boys. Other critics discuss the problematic aspect of an operational definition of self-concept. Although psychologists measure self-esteem, a measurable definition of self-concept (to predict delinquency) remains unavailable. Finally, the most damaging criticism of containment theory is that it does not work. Reckless and Dintz (1972) conducted a four-year project to enhance the self-concept of junior high age boys. Historical analysis indicated little impact on long-term delinquency.

Beccaria s Deterrence Doctrine

Deterrence doctrine represents the oldest, the most influential, and in many ways the most interesting of the social control theories. Today, most texts only mention deterrence doctrine because of its historical significance. Partly because of the problematic aspect of proving that something was deterred or did not happen, research appears sporadic and haphazard. Few modern theorists accept deterrence doctrine as an explanation for control of criminal behavior. The public however cries for stiffer criminal penalties, more police, and more prisons as an answer to crime. I find this interesting and paradoxical. To fully develop the flavor of deterrence doctrine requires a discussion of the historical setting, the principal author, impact of the theory, problems with the approach, and recent research to address these concerns.

I present general criminology from the perspective of three schools of thought. The demonology school, the oldest, assumes that people commit crimes because some evil spirit possesses them. Examples include the nineteen witches burned in Salem, Massachusetts in 1692. Deterrence doctrine, or the classical school, began in the mid 1600s and today enjoys popular support mostly outside academia. Examples of popular support include the continued building of prisons and modern support for stiffer criminal penalties and capital punishment. The positivist school, the most modern, assumes behavior is determined by forces generally beyond the control of the individual. These forces may be either biological, psychological, social forces or others. Examples from the positive school include the work of Hirschi (1969) and Reckless (1973).

Many criminologists accept the classical school as the beginning of modern criminology. The classical school assumes that people commit crimes after weighing the consequences of their actions. In the classical model, the fear of a particular punishment deters people from committing a particular crime. The classical school emerged entirely from the publication of a short work by Cesar Beccaria (1764). To fully understand this work requires an appreciation of its setting.

The enlightenment period had just begun in Europe. This brought forth ideas of rationalism, liberalism, humanitarian and scientific thought. Examples in England include the development in 1701 of the grain drill that suddenly made food more available. By 1700, London housed over 450,000 people. London grew in spite of fire and plague to a population of over 550,000 by 1760. In 1760, steam engines powered coal smelting for steel and textile spinning equipment. That same year, the English began digging over 2,000 miles of canals to support London s economy, the largest in Europe (Spartacus Encyclopedia, 2000).

World changes occurred. Later in the 1700s, Prussia began a military conquest that ultimately doubled its size. Austria warred against Germany. In the American Colonies, Boston and Philadelphia boasted 12,000 residents each. New York contained a population of 5,000. The 262,000 people of the American colonies would grow to over 3,000,000 by 1770, primarily by immigration from Britain, Germany and the Netherlands (North American History, 2000).

Marx, Durkheim, Weber, Freud, Darwin, Comte, and the French Revolution all followed this period. Criminal behavior was thought of as crimes against the State, crimes against the Church or crimes against the Crown. Laws found their beginnings in tradition and local customs. Most laws were never written. Most people could not read. Different laws applied to different social classes. Judges invoked punishment for unheard-of laws and monarchs simply imprisoned. Punishments included branding, burning, flogging, mutilation, drowning, banishment, beheading and hanging. In England, for example, over two hundred offenses including pick-pocketing and shoplifting carried capital punishments. In France an accused person could be suspended from his/her limbs and weights placed on his chest until he either confessed or died. Many people died during this interrogation. The choice to confess brought a swift death, but also meant forfeiture of family lands and possessions to the church or crown from a confessed criminal. Cesare Beccaria grew up and studied law in this social setting (Pfohl, 1994).

Cesare Bonesana, Marchese di Beccaria was born the eldest son to an aristocratic Italian family in 1738. In 1758, Beccaria received a law degree from the University of Pavia. After graduation, he married a woman from a lower social class against the strong wishes of his family. He then met Pictro Verri and joined a local men s activists group, the Academy of Fist. At the urging of Verri and the Academy, Beccaria researched and published On Crime and Punishment in 1764. He developed and never overcame a public shyness. Nevertheless, the times were right; his book brought world attention and support (Pfohl, Stephen, 1994).[5]

The work distinguished between sin and crime, between politics and religion. It urged limiting the wealth, influence, and authority of the clergy. It rejected the military authority of the landed aristocracy and encouraged a competitive commercial society. Beccaria encouraged the concept of personal economic gain and a higher personal standard of living. From this development emerged the concept of equality before the law. Beccaria described the law as impersonal, a pact among free men. The law should be mild and humane. Torture does not determine truth; it violates the right to self-defense, and should be eliminated.

Like torture, the death penalty should also be eliminated. He wrote that it is less of a deterrent to crime than hard labor; it violates the right to self-protection; and it gives too much power to the court. Beccaria envisioned a system where only legislators created laws and judges imposed punishment only in accordance with the written law. Most important, Beccaria made the following points:

- Punishment should be based on the individual act, not the actor;
- Punishment should be determined by the crime;
- Punishment should be prompt and effective;
- It is better to prevent crime than to punish it.

Beccaria s influence spread worldwide. Voltaire referred to Beccaria as his brother and wrote the introduction to Beccaria s French edition. In 1791, following the French Revolution, this work became the guide for rewriting the French Penal Code. Russia s Catherine the Great ordered the work translated into Russian and studied. Prussia s Frederick the Great revised both his civil and criminal code based on Beccaria s writings. Austria s Joseph in 1787 also drafted a new criminal code that for the first time abolished capital punishment. Beccaria's name is even frequently mentioned in the debate minutes during the writing of the U.S. Bill of Rights (Pfohl, Stephen, 1994).[6]

One aspect of the wide acceptance of Beccaria s work is its simplicity. People are rational thinkers who weigh the consequences of their actions. Jeremy Bentham (1789) referred to this as the pleasure or pain principle and the rationalization process as hedonistic calculus. Bentham went on to say that certainty outweighed severity as a deterrent to crime and that the pain from committing a crime should be only slightly more costly than the pleasure from breaking the same law.

In summary, deterrence doctrine assumes people to be rational thinkers. As such, the fear of punishment for a particular crime deters people from committing that crime. Finally, the deterrent effect of punishment depends upon its certainty, celerity (swiftness) and severity.

Figure 1
Beccaria s Deterrence Model

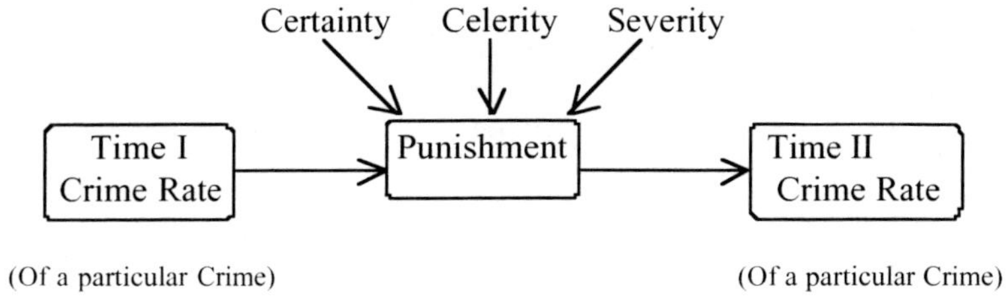

Within Beccaria s model, crime rate, or the potential for an individual to commit a particular crime, becomes the dependent variable. This rational-thought decision process on the part of the individual to commit the crime is based on the independent variable, punishment. Fear of punishment becomes the mechanism that drives the model. Certainty, celerity and severity become various dimensions of the concept of punishment.

The model suggests that as the fear of the certainty, celerity, or severity of punishment increases, the rate for that particular crime decrease. The model fails to explain a relationship between certainty, celerity and severity. Finally, there survives no evidence that Beccaria attempted to test his model.

Although logical, this model provides problems for modern researchers. Where does the fear of punishment originate? How is fear learned or transmitted? Do measures of deterrence measure fear of punishment, moral condemnation of crime, or some other spurious value? Must certainty, celerity, and severity all be present for fear to drive the model? Do these dimensions act independently or collectively?

The theory also fails to differentiate between juveniles and adults, between the sane and the mentally ill, and consider social forces such as poverty, alienation and social status. What about the otherwise non-criminal who, for example, steals food to ward off starvation? Again, research does not test the assumption that fear of punishment decreases crime. This leaves a theory with inferred validity.

Gibbs (1976) argues that deterrence is not a theory at all. (Deterrence doctrine is) a vague congery of ideas with no unifying factor other than their being the legacies of two major figures in moral philosophy (Beccaria and Bentham) . Gibbs idea of deterrence approaches theory by reducing deterrence to what he calls its most basic generalization, The rate for a particular type of crime varies inversely with the certainty, celerity and severity of punishment of that type of crime. Even within this model, formulating testable hypothesis remains difficult.

Gibbs (1976) recognizes that deterrence is not directly measurable. Gibbs asks, If the reader has not killed today, does this result from the deterrent effect of the death penalty, internalized norms, something learned from family and peers or simply a lack of opportunity? Likewise, must a penalty be previously experienced, known of or simply perceived, to be a deterrent of crime?

Other criticisms of the classical school involve the concept of rational choice. By making deviate behavior a rational choice, society faults the offender. Society is no longer to blame and there is no longer a need for social reform. If the offender is to blame, punishment becomes rationalized as just desserts. Feeling better than those people in prison enhances individuals self-esteem. Prison labor becomes an economical alternative to the cost of prison training and education programs. This may explain the long time public support for deterrence ideology.

Modern research to answer these questions generally falls within one of three categories or within three periods of research. The first set of research examines objective information, generally in the form of historical analysis of existing data. Researchers within this tradition compare and contrast crime rates and length of incarceration for a specific crime. They look, for example, at homicide or rape rates and numbers of executions for each of these crimes. They may also compare crime rates to police clearance rates or any combination of existing data. Researchers within this tradition include Wellford (1974), Erickson and Gibbs (1968), Schiraldi and Godfrey (1995), Lieberman (1994, 1995), Gibbs (1975), and Tittle and Rowe (1974).

An example of this research is the work of Lamson, Crowther, Spacy and Crump (1968). Lamson et al. questioned the historical impact of criminal penalties in the United States. They conducted a historical analysis of crime rates for specific offenses compared to the median time offenders actually served for committing the same offense. The researchers reviewed data for forty-eight states and a number of serious and non-violent crimes.

Lamson et al. (1968) concluded that there is no significant relation between crime rate and prison time served and that there is no evidence that prison rehabilitates. Finally, the authors found no correlation between length of incarceration and recidivism.

The second set of research examines perceptual data. This research usually encompasses either a survey or in-depth interview methodology. It examines concepts like perceived penalties for a particular crime, perceived length of prison sentences and estimated chances of being caught for committing a crime. The research relies heavily on self-reported criminal activity and individual perceptions of the self as well as the generalized other. Researchers within this tradition include Meier and Johnson (1977), Piliavin, Gartner, Thornton, and Matsueda (1986), Cook (1980), Glassner, Ksander, Berg, and Johnson (1983), Miller (1968), Silberman (1976), Klepper and Nagin (1989), and Paternoster, Saltzman, Chiticos and Waldo (1982).

Anderson, Chiricos and Waldo (1977) provide an example of perceptual research that questioned the relative and cumulative impact of perceived informal and formal sanctions upon self-reported marijuana use among university students. The researchers used a structured personal interview questionnaire with a Likert-type scale response and asked users and non-users questions about perceived formal sanctions like how likely are you to get caught for smoking marijuana; what is the penalty? They also asked users and non-users questions about perceived informal sanctions like what is your family s (friend s) attitude toward marijuana; what is your perceived usage by your friends?

Anderson Chiricos and Waldo (1977) found that perceived severity of formal punishment is unrelated to reported marijuana use. Their survey also showed that severe punishment is not as strong a deterrent as certain punishment and that severe punishment becomes more of a deterrent among those offenders most certain of being caught. The researchers concluded that perceived informal sanctions are a greater deterrent (especially among peers) than perceived formal sanctions. They also concluded that the cumulative impact of certainty and perceived informal sanctions are greater than the additive impact of certainty and perceived informal sanctions alone and that formal and informal deterrent effects are slightly greater for males than for females.

The third set of research focuses on changes over time. Many of these studies use a panel design and examine the relationship between life experiences and future criminal behavior. Researchers within this tradition include: Green (1989), and Paternoster, Saltzman, Waldo, and Chiricos (1983).

An example from this tradition is Smith and Gartin (1989). These researchers examined arrests, as a form of punishment, reduce or increase subsequent criminal activity using a longitudinal cohort study of males born in 1949, until age 25. They found that the more times police contacted an individual on a violation, the more likely that the officer would arrest the individual. More importantly, they found that 50 percent of those arrested on their first contact with police were not contacted again.

Smith and Gartin (1989) concluded that the more contacts with police, the more likely there would be future contacts after the second contact. Moreover, the deterrent effects of arrest operate differently on novice and experienced offenders (less effective on experienced).

Researchers also explored the three dimensions of Beccaria s concept of punishment. Tittle and Rowe (1974) found that the certainty of punishment needed to be 30 percent to be effective. Bailey (1976) found that certainty should be 50 percent. Finally, Wilson and McLaren (1977) without supporting research suggest that that traffic police should issue 18 traffic tickets for each fatality accident to be effective. Wilson and McLaren believe that more aggressive ticket writing only serves to increase revenue and fails to significantly impact the accident rate.

Beccaria (1764) and Bentham (1789) both felt that severity was the least effective dimension of punishment. Berk and Newton (1985) found that arresting (a punishment) men for domestic violence opposed to ordering the abuser to leave the premise (a warning) significantly decreases future acts of domestic abuse. However, Sellin (1967) found that capital punishment does not significantly deter murder. Miller (1968) reported that people generally do not even know what the punishment is for most common serious crimes. Gibbs (1976) discovered a high correlation between certainty of punishment and deterrence, but a poor correlation between severity of punishment and deterrence with respect to homicide rates. Finally, Schiraldi and Godfrey (1995) found that murder rates increased during periods when more executions for murder took place in California.

Bentham (1789) also thought that swift punishment brought the most pain. Jacoby (1978) agreed that swift punishment is a better deterrent for crime but current systems of criminal justice prohibit swift punishment. Meier and Johnson (1977) also theorized that swift punishment is a greater deterrent but that police are hindered by the court system and only judges can improve the deterrent effect of the system. Unfortunately, none of these authors provided research to support their positions.

Cognition

All social control theories depend on some assumed degree of individual rational thought. Many commonly accepted concepts of rational thought take one of many forms of psychological classical conditioning, operant psychology or vicarious learning. These include habituation, conditioned reflex, extinction, generalization, discrimination, operant behavior, instrumental conditioning and many others.

One dimension of classical conditioning involves the dualistic nature of the stimulus and the response. This represents an isolatable and independent cause which provides explanation for a subsequent action called the effect. The clearest criticism of this explanation is provided by Watts (1957) in his discussion of Zen Buddhism: An observer peers through a gap in the wall to watch a line of passing cats. Because he always sees the whiskers first and the tails last, and there are never tails without whiskers, the observer concludes that whiskers cause tails.

John Dewey (1896) provides a more social psychological explanation of rational thought. Dewey explains rational thought by a process that he calls the reflex arc. Dewey further describes this process as a patchwork of disjointed perceptual, thought and behavioral processes. These processes are not distinct, but operate as a single concrete whole, continuously folding over each other, a process of coordination.

In the reflex arc, the human receiver within the context of previous experiences and current situations interprets stimulus. Data is constantly being accepted and reevaluated, but most importantly interpreted. In this description, sound becomes less a stimulus as much as a process of hearing. This involves everything from the movement and position of the head to recognition of, or creation of, a symbolic representation of a word. Should the word be recognized as fire, for example, the reflex arc continues through the process of running away, a process seen as much more involved that a distinct stimulus response interpretation. This constant assessment also allows for generalizations of stimulus and response. For example, where similar but not exact situations or stimulus occurs, a generalized response become available by folding back upon a similar situation. In other words, if I got in trouble for lying, I might also get in trouble for stealing. I combine Dewey s (1896) concept of the reflex arc with Bandura s (1986) social learning theory for what I call cognition.

Bandura (1986) saw social learning occurring in four distinct steps. First, the actor observes or pays attention to some social occurrence. This may involve either witnessing an arrest on the street or participating in gossip concerning the same event. Next, the information becomes coded in a cognitive process that relates the information to past experience or a new or previously established category of information. Learning depends on an individual ability to perform the previously observed and categorized information. Finally, reinforcements for the behavior emerges either from outside or inside the individual and may involve action, or the decision not to act given a similar situation or stimulus. In this way, cognition involves a more comprehensive process than decision making implied by the term rational thought.

In conclusion, social control theories share that some type of control is necessary to prevent deviant behavior. The theories differ in types of control mechanisms and what these controls effect. Many critics complain that social control only addresses small juvenile groups and minor crime (Thio, 1988). This may result from the self-report studies that contribute to much of the earliest social control research. Supporting these critics, Hirschi (1969) tested his theories on schoolchildren. Reckless (1973) tested his theory on sixth-grade boys. Replication studies by Wiatrowski, Griswald and Roberts (1981) and Krohn and Massey (1980) also used self-report surveys and failed to resolve these criticisms. Even research on deterrence theory proves inconsistent. Theories of cognition and learning provide an explanation of how the information for social and individual action is received, processed and acted upon.

Research, therefore, is needed for an expansion of social control and cognition to adult serious crime. Research can also generalize deterrence theory. Past research examines the deterrent effect of punishment for a particular crime on either personal concepts or recidivism for that particular offense. Research has not generalized the effect of punishment for one offence as a deterrent effect for committing other non-related crimes. Research can also provide application to the sociological problem of drinking and serious crime, and explanations for the successes of many modern community-policing programs that take credit for recent drops in rates of serious crime (see Table 1). The following model addresses many of these concerns.

NOTES

[1] Psychological, nutritional, and biological perspectives of deviance are some of the many exceptions. See Diana H. Fishbein, Biological Perspectives in Criminology, Criminology 28 (1990): 27-40 and Stephen Schoenthaler, Diet and Crime: An empirical examination of the value of nutrition in the control and treatment of incarcerated juvenile offenders, International Journal of Biosocial Research 4 (1982): 25-39 and Semore L. Halleck, Psychiatry and the Dilemmas of Crime, New York: Harper and Row, 1967.

[2] Although a common theme in Hobbs writings, this citation comes from the philosopher s response, Hobbs, Thomas. 1681. (Edited by Cropsey, Joseph. 1971). A Dialogue Between A Philosopher and A Student Of The Common Laws Of England. University of Chicago Press. Chicago. p. 122.

[3] For more information concerning replication studies see, Jennifer Friedman & Dennis P. Rosenbaum, Social Control Theory: The salience of components by age, gender, and type of crime, Journal of Quantitative Criminology, 4, 1988: 363-381. and Michael J. Hindelang, Causes of Delinquency: A partial replication and extension, Social Problems, 20, 1973: 471-487.

[4] Modern examples for providing alternative behavior include programs such as D.A.R.E. (Drug Awareness Resistance Education), G.R.E.A.T. (Gang Resistance Education And Training), and Just Say No To Drugs.

[5] See Pfohl, Stephen, 1994, for a more extensive background to the culture, social setting and economic development or 18th Century Europe at the time of Beccaria.

[6] This entire section relies heavily on the historical account provided by Pfohl, Stephen, 1994, particularly his historical and developmental description of the period.

CHAPTER 3

A Model of Social Control

My model is based on the observation that serious crime tends to decrease when people are prohibited from drinking beer on public streets and sidewalks. The model explains the relationship between almost insignificant punishments for a nuisance offense to a variety of seemingly unrelated serious crimes.

If successful, the model predicts and explains the decrease in index crimes following enforcement of nuisance laws such as: drunkenness, vagrancy, begging, junk vehicles, code violations and others. The model also provides explanation for the success of police foot patrol, mounted units and other community policing and aggressive preventative patrol activities. Finally, the model explains the failure of significant impacts of simply passing another law without enforcement and penalty and the failure of increasing penalties and jail sentences as a means to reduce rates of serious crimes.

Assumptions

I make the following assumptions in developing a social control model of criminal behavior:

1. To varying degrees all individuals possess self-serving agendas which sometime violate social norms;
2. People are capable of voluntary self-direction;

3. Index (serious) crimes are universal; people know that violating index crimes violates both formal and informal social norms and carry social sanctions;
4. Cognition/decisions/behavior-generating-mechanisms take place on various levels of consciousness;
5. An individual s perception of getting caught and punished for criminal behavior depends on social myth, personal experience, inductive and deductive logic;
6. People create the environment to which they react;
7. People do not share equal levels of cognition (i.e. children, mentally ill, unusual circumstances/environment, poverty, social status, alienation, and others);
8. Behavior becomes predictable when the consequences of actions are obvious, certain, immediate, and with some degree of severity attached;
9. The decision to violate social norms depends on the certainty, celerity, and severity of the consequences of that behavior;
10. Certainty, celerity, and severity of punishment act both independently and additively; certainty and celerity are most important, severity is least important, but necessary;
11. The act of being contacted and cited by police especially in the presence of others constitutes some form of punishment.

Figure 2
Conceptual Social Control Model of Criminal Behavior[1]

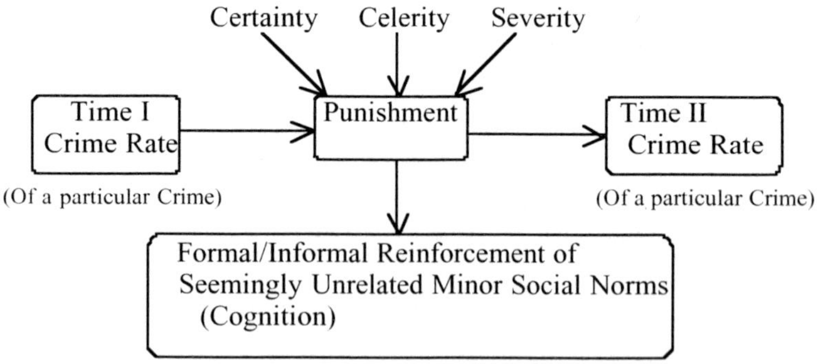

Rationale

Like all social control models, I assume that deviance is a natural human condition. Sometimes norm-abiding people break traffic laws, talk with their mouth full or, less commonly today, fail to take their hat off when they enter an elevator. Maybe it is how we test and reinforce social boundaries. Maybe it is a biological natural selection process. Maybe it is how we socially evolve. Whatever the rhyme or reason, it occurs.

Socialization becomes the collective formal and informal social control forces that either permit or control these natural deviant occurrences. The police represent the most immediate and visible forms of formal social control. Friends and peer groups represent informal social controls. In the case of public drinking, bar owners, managers, bouncers and doorpersons fall somewhere between formal and informal agents of social control.

A major criticism of Hirschi (1969) is the inclusiveness of his list of social bonds. This does not matter. As individuals, we all form a unique set of social bonds each with their own strengths and weaknesses. It is our individual commitment to and ownership of our bonds that form our inner and outer pushes and pulls that Reckless (1973) discusses. This internalized package becomes the self.

As norms, values and belief systems become internalized, cognition occurs on both the conscious and preconscious levels. A poorly developed belief system against violence, for example, might be strong enough to keep a person from hitting the boss following a poor evaluation received in the mail (cognition on the conscious level). The same belief system may fail to prevent domestic abuse when it occurs under the influence of high emotion and substance abuse (diminished cognition on a preconscious level) in the perceived privacy of one s home.

Deterrence drives this socialization by cognition. If every time (certainty) a man fails to take off his hat when he enters an elevator, he receives immediate (celerity) disapproving looks (severity), the custom of hat removal would continue. Changing gender roles in western society remove the certainty, celerity and severity of punishment for a man failing to open a door for a woman; this custom is dying.[2]

Traditionally deterrence addressed a specific crime and a specific punishment for that crime. Deterrence traditionally represents a micro process operating on the individual level. I believe that by looking at deterrence as a dimension of cognition which in turn drives the socialization process we can further generalize the deterrence model.

Police enforce a wide range of formal social controls, the legal code. If police enforce minor nuisance laws with certainty, celerity, and some (minor yet measurable) degree of severity, this deterrent effect should generalize and reinforce the rational thought process against committing more serious crimes. For example, if a person is arrested for begging immediately and every time s/he begs, that person is less likely to commit a robbery than a person who frequently begs without negative consequences. It is within this framework that I operationalize my model.

Predictions

This conceptual model of social control of criminal behavior provides a number of predictions. First, actual and/or perceived formal and/or informal, specific and/or general punishment must be present to drive the model. Punishment functions together with cognition. As punishment is experienced and/or perceived, thought, learning and generalization folds back upon themselves to reinforce deterrence of future criminal behavior.

For deterrence to occur, there must be a degree of certainty, celerity, and severity present to drive the folding-back or reinforcement aspect of punishment. Dimensions of punishment emerge from various types of social controls. These may be formal in the form of police, security personnel or bouncers in bars and taverns. Social controls may also come from informal sources such as strangers, friends or social settings. Social controls therefore represent real and observable social facts.

I predict that the greater the certainty and celerity, with minimal but appropriately severe punishment, the greater the deterrence effect on criminal behavior. Social control and environmental situations contribute to this area. Cognition determines the degree and source of punishment dependent upon the environmental, social setting and the individual. For example, inside a bar, admonishment from a peer may have the same deterrent effect as arrest and jail for the same infraction on a street or sidewalk (assuming the same certainty and celerity of action).

Finally, the model generalizes crime and punishment. Certainty and celerity of appropriately severe punishment reduces incidences of future otherwise unrelated crime.

From an applied perspective:

a) If a nuisance law is present and not enforced then no change in index crime rate occurs;
b) If a nuisance law is present and enforced without minimal significant penalty then no change in index crime rate occurs;
c) If a nuisance law is present and enforced with minimal significant penalty then significant change in index crime rate occurs.

These predictions lead to a hypothesis of deterrence, social control, and reduction of serious criminal behavior.

Hypothesis

Crime statistics indicate that some degree of serious crimes occur regardless of prohibitions against drinking beer on streets, sidewalks and in public areas. Sociological research literature suggests that social controls can be identified which may act through rationalization and influence criminal behavior. Therefore, my hypothesis states that serious crime decreases with the increase in perceived social control through the enforcement of nuisance laws such as prohibitions against public beer drinking. In other words, enforcing, with minor but measurable penalties, prohibitions against public beer drinking should decrease serious crime.

NOTES

[1]Within this model, the dependent variable becomes crime rate, the independent variable becomes punishment, and the mechanism to drive the model, cognition.

[2] Reinforcement also involves the concept of conditioned response learning, which contains different dimensions from the concept of the rational thought process and is not addressed here.

CHAPTER 4

Methodology

Research Objective and Strategy

This research consists of a single objective. I attempt to explain the rate of serious crime by the enforcement of a nuisance ordinance prohibiting the public consumption of beer. Social control theory provides a reasonable explanation if adult serious crime is decreased by enforced prohibitions against public drinking. Enforcement, explained by deterrence theory, drives the model. To test this hypothesis, communities prohibiting the public consumption of beer must be identified. Comparisons of crime rates before and after enacting and enforcing such legislation provide one indicator of social control. Conducting ethnographic studies of these communities and non-participant observation of drinking behavior inside and outside bars and taverns should provide others. These data can then be compared to similar communities allowing public consumption of beer.

Actual and perceived social controls must be identified inside bars and taverns and at the same time, absent or diminished outside bars, on streets and sidewalks and public areas to account for significant differences in serious crime. Furthermore, for deterrence to operationalize, the social control model, there must be some form of certainty, celerity and severity of punishment for violating these social norms (i.e. laws). This study will identify and contrast those social control agents occurring inside bars and restaurants to social dynamics occurring on streets and sidewalks and at the same time examine the effectiveness of deterrence to operationalize the model.

Figure 3
Methods Summary

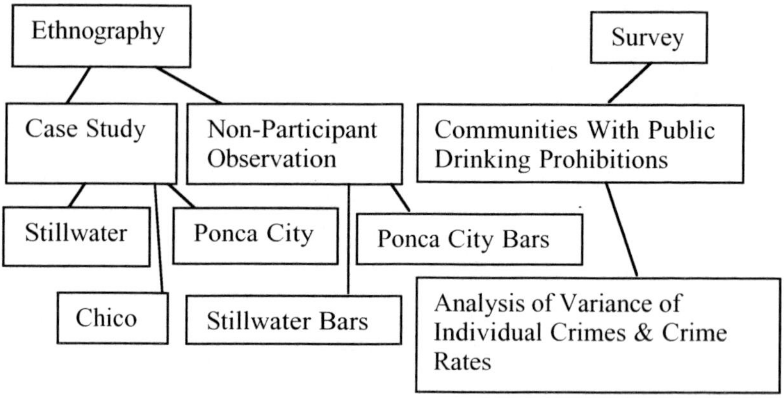

The research began with a case study of Stillwater, Oklahoma and the development and life history of two street parties. I selected Stillwater because of its close proximity and my familiarity with the community and the events surrounding two Stillwater street parties. Stillwater reacted to each street party by enacting a public drinking prohibition. The first street party slowly died. Stillwater enforced the ordinance for four years, and then repealed the law in a referendum election. This allows before, during and after comparisons of crime data.

Several years later, another street party began. Stillwater resurrected the public drinking ban and the second party abruptly ended. The second event allows before and after comparisons of crime data and a comparison of the effectiveness of each of the two public drinking prohibitions within the same community setting. This data is presented both as ethnography of the community and events and by tables and statistical analysis illustrating changes in the rate of serious crime before and after enacting public beer drinking prohibitions.

Methods also include identifying a population and creating a list of licensed Stillwater bars. The Stillwater City Clerk issues local annual licenses and provided information for this list. With the list, I developed a typology or classification scheme of types of bars and taverns. These include the neighborhood bar, the theme bar, the hotel bar and the restaurant bar. I visited each Stillwater bar then categorized each bar into one of the established bar-types. After visiting and categorizing each bar, I selected a single bar as an ideal-type of each particular category and conducted non-participant observation of culture, group and individual activity in and around the bar.

The non-participant observation seeks to identify those social controls present inside specific types of bars and taverns which are similar, different or absent outside of bars and/or on public property. I compared these social controls between one community who prohibits public consumption of beer (Stillwater) to a similar community who allows public beer drinking (Ponca City).

I selected Ponca City, Oklahoma as a second site for non-participant observation. Ponca City was selected because of its close proximity and similarity to Stillwater except that Ponca City has never prohibited the public consumption of beer. The Ponca City study also uses an ethnographic methodology and includes the history, culture and demographics of the community. I selected those descriptors that seem important, unique and which provide the best thick description of the culture and the people of the town.

I also obtained a listing of licensed bars in Ponca City. I visited each bar and classified the bar using the same typology used in the Stillwater study. I then selected an ideal-type bar from each category and conducted non-participant observation in each of the ideal-type bars selected.

An additional method involved quantifying the actual influence of public drinking prohibitions on serious crime. This began by identifying communities with public drinking prohibitions. I reviewed copies of municipal ordinances at the Oklahoma Bar Association, used Internet mailing lists and wrote letters to identify communities that prohibit public beer drinking. Once identified, I established a list of communities that prohibit public drinking. From the list, I eliminated those communities with reported crime rates less than three years before and three years after enacting their public beer drinking prohibitions. I eliminated those communities who report their crime data commingled with another agency like the county sheriff s office. I also eliminated those communities that report using the NIBRIS (National Incident Reporting System) rather than the UCR (Uniform Crime Reporting) system.

With these data, I conducted an analysis of variance seeking significance between crime rates before and after enacting individual communities public drinking prohibition. Interestingly, I found significance in the first Stillwater data, little significance in the second Stillwater data and significance in a community similar to Stillwater, Chico, California.

Finding unexpected data, the methodology became more inductive. I then conducted an additional ethnography of Chico, California. I specifically examined the community, the culture and a life history of a local street party in Chico and the party s associated violence. I concluded the methodology by comparing and contrasting the reaction of Chico and Stillwater to their street party experiences and the apparent impact of these actions on serious crime. Finally, I used these data to fold back upon the general research objective and place the data within the theoretical research model.

Ethnographies

I conducted the ethnographic study of Stillwater, Ponca City, and Chico following the format used by Gans (1962) study of an urban community and Kotarba s (1984) study of drinking and driving experiences of tavern regulars. This provided rich detail about the culture of the community and the street party experiences in Stillwater and Chico. This also provided insight into perceived social controls present when groups drink in streets, sidewalks and on public property both in communities who allow and prohibit public beer drinking.

I collected data by examining newspapers and media reports, police reports, government Internet sites, minutes from city commission meetings and other government documents. I used these sources to determine how policy decisions are made, who makes those decisions and why. Police reports and government documents are known and available through the Oklahoma Open Records Act and the

Federal Freedom of Information Act (Amdur, 1963).[1] Personal notes taken by reporters during the Stillwater events were obtained because of long time working relationships, trust and informed consent. I identified social controls present inside bars and taverns in Stillwater and Ponca City by non-participant observation.

In total, I spent over 100 hours of non-participant observation of drinking behavior inside and around bars, restaurants and other areas where people congregate and drink. This added to the ethnography by comparing and contrasting attitudes, values and belief systems as well as behavior of individuals drinking inside bars to those drinking in public areas. Data is presented as a thick description (Geertz, 1973) of culture and drinking behavior within the community. I used these data to identify the origins and effectiveness of perceived and actual social controls present inside bars, taverns and restaurants to those present on streets and sidewalks.

I selected Ponca City to represent communities who allow public beer drinking because of Ponca s proximity and similarity to Stillwater.[2] I made every effort to examine Ponca City in the same way as I studied Stillwater. I present Ponca City data as rich detail to support or refute the Stillwater data.

Survey

To examine directly the relationship between public beer drinking and serious crime, I identified several communities that prohibit public drinking by local ordinance. Once identified, I collected crime rates from Uniform Crime Reports.[3] I then compared crime rates before and after enacting individual ordinances by analysis of variance. I encountered problems identifying communities with public drinking prohibitions.

There exists no listing of local laws for communities within the State of Oklahoma. To establish a population, I contacted several organizations for help. They included: the Oklahoma Bar Association, The Oklahoma Sheriff s and Peace Officer s Association, the

Oklahoma District Attorney s Training Council, The Oklahoma Municipal League and various computer bulletin board postings. My population ultimately contained communities inside and outside Oklahoma. For example I received an e-mail from an official at the Oklahoma Bar Association saying that he heard that several Big-8 NCAA Conference communities also prohibited public beer drinking. Other contacts identified other communities outside Oklahoma. I collected data on every community identified. I eliminated only those communities who either:

1. Did not have available both three years of crime data before enacting their public drinking prohibition and three years of crime data after enacting their public drinking prohibition;
2. Had their crime data commingled with another department, like an adjoining larger city, or the county sheriff s office;
3. Used a crime reporting system other than the Federal Bureau of Investigation (FBI) Uniform Crime Reporting (UCR) system.

Once I identified a community that prohibits public beer drinking, I contacted the city court clerk, city attorney or police department for a copy of their public drinking ordinance. After receiving the ordinances, I verified the date of enactment/enforcement with the local community.[4] I then obtained published UCR crime data on the particular community.

With this information, I compared rates of individual crimes before and after enacting public drinking prohibitions within selected communities. I recorded this information as overall crime rates and rates of each of the individual UCR Part I Offences. This further identified the particular type of crime most impacted by public drinking prohibitions.

Non-Participant Observation

I begin the non-participant observation by obtaining a list of licensed establishments (bars) in Stillwater and Ponca City. In Stillwater, the list came from the City Clerk. In Ponca City, the list came from the Utilities Authority.

The Stillwater list contained 112 licensed establishments. I eliminated gas stations, convenience stores, catering businesses, grocery stores, fraternal organizations and delivery services.[5] Because my interest is specifically beer drinking, I eliminated those mixed beverage establishments which only sell hard liquor. Retail liquor stores did not appear on the list and were not considered. After visiting each of the remaining 39 bars, I divided them into the four established categories. I purposely selected one bar from each category. I selected bars based on representativeness to each category, the presence of a well-defined curtilage or outside public drinking area and their volume of business. For example, I visited one hotel bar that never had more than two customers. This bar was not selected.

I followed the same procedure in selecting representative bars in Ponca City. The Ponca City list originally contained 64 licensed establishments. Of these, 51 sold only beer and 13 sold beer and mixed beverages. After eliminating grocery stores, gas stations, catering businesses, fraternal organizations and two bars that are closed for remodeling, I considered 35 bars. As in Stillwater, I visited each of these bars and selected those bars that appeared most representative of each category. Within the categories I made the final selection based on the bars with the largest number of customers.

Bar Classifications

I found no available descriptive classification system for bars and taverns in the referenced literature. As I visited each of the Stillwater bars, I talked with the bar employees and customers. I asked employees how they would describe their bar. I examined the motif of wall, furniture and other decorations. I asked customers why they enjoy and visit this particular bar and about other bars that they patronize. I visited with neighbors and passerby s about what they thought about the bar. I also visited with police officers working the bar beat and asked them to describe particular bars. Finally, I examined individual motivations concerning why people go to bars, and various types of sociological classification schemes.

Finding no reference literature, I classified bars into four types based primarily on the culture of the bar and the individual motivation and needs of those who patronize the business. My classification types include the hotel/motel bars, the restaurant bars, the theme bar, and the neighborhood bar. I described individual classifications more fully in Chapter I, Definition of Terms.

Ethical Considerations

These research procedures address several ethical considerations. Only documents that are voluntarily provided or within the public record were reviewed. Individuals either contacted or observed were not deceived in any way. No attempt was made to identify any of the individuals observed. The identities of those individuals known and observed were kept private and confidential. Research subjects received no compensation (other than the researcher s thanks) for participation in this study. There was no outside funding associated with this project.

Research topics were neither particularly sensitive nor personal. Research data did not contain offensive or threatening material or content. There was no particular physical or psychological anxiety or stress associated with this research. Informed consent was used with everyone contacted about this project.

Validity and Reliability

This study combines various theories of social control, deterrence, rational thought and learning into a model that explains reducing rates of serious crime by enforcing local laws prohibiting the public consumption of beer. The model generalizes from the data and predicts reductions in serious crime by enforcing other nuisance laws such as junk cars, begging and code violations. It also explains the success of many community policing efforts. This chapter discusses the validity, reliability and study strengths of this effort.

Validity describes the degree to which data or measures accurately reflect the concept intended to be measured (Katzen, Cook and Crouch, 1991). External or construct validity increases by using a variety of methodologies. This technique uses Denzin s (1989) concept of triangulation. In this way, one concept is operationalized in a number of ways. Validity increases with similarity of research data.

I addressed external validity by conducting a survey of before and after crime rates of communities who enacted public drinking laws. I then statistically compared crime rates before and after enacting the public drinking ordinance and evaluated the results. I also conducted ethnographic case studies of two communities with public drinking prohibitions and one community that never restricted public drinking. Finally, I conducted non-participant observation of drinking behavior in and around bars in one community that prohibited public drinking and one community where public drinking was allowed. Although the different methods addressed various dimensions of the concept of public drinking and serious crime, the variety of methods used also enhanced the external validity of the study.

Internal validity or item analysis asks if the methods used influence the data obtained. Put another way, internal validity asks if other methods were used, would this result in the same outcomes and conclusions. This study avoids many internal validity problems by the type of methods involved. This study did not influence the previously occurred and published crime rates of the communities surveyed. Case studies used historical accounts from government documents, newspapers and police reports. Before and after testing of human subjects did not prejudice research results. I possibly influenced non-participant observation data by my presence inside bars and taverns. I compensated for this possibility by repeated visits to the same bar taking notice that my presence became either accepted or ignored by regular customers.

Finally, this study originated within an academic setting as a doctoral dissertation. As such, a committee of academic professionals reviewed the proposal and methodology. Others reviewed the study s impact on human subjects. These reviews by panels of experts increased the face validity of the project.

Reliability relates to results and measures remaining constant and reproducible over time. I enhanced reliability by surveying a variety of communities with public drinking prohibitions. These communities represented a variety of locations. The communities enacted their public drinking prohibitions at different times. These issues increase reliability.

Non-participant methodology to observe social controls inside bars raises reliability concerns. I partially addressed these concerns by providing a sample of my non-participation observation methodology to Bob Morgan. Morgan is a Ph.D. student studying psychology at Oklahoma State University. Morgan also conducted non-participant observation of drinking behavior inside and outside of some of the same bars that I researched. Morgan found similar behavior and drew similar conclusions within the same type bars as I. This increased reliability; more researchers and observations would further increase the project reliability.

Independent researchers classifying individual bars into the established types could also enhance reliability. These procedures became resource prohibitive for this project. Next I discuss some of these validity and reliability issues as strengths and weaknesses of the study and opportunities for continued research.

Study Strengths

I expected widespread computerization of police records but did not find it! Even many large police departments only maintain records on those index crimes required to be reported by federal law. Local data concerning charges and arrests for minor offenses was obtained by subjective recall and observation by police officers, court clerks and clerical staff. Data quality represents a limitation to analysis and conclusions based on this type information. As computerization becomes more widely used by small and medium size law enforcement agencies, more exact data will become available.

Another limitation emerged with the classification of Ponca City bars. I classified Ponca City bars by visiting each bar. Some bars were closed for either remodeling or had gone out of business. Of the remaining bars, classifications were generally made during a fifteen to thirty minute visit. I assessed the structure, the neighborhood, the decorations and the people. In other words, I assessed the culture, the setting and the attitudes, values and belief systems of the people.

There was little problem in Stillwater where I possessed a rich background of the community and the bars. In Ponca City, classifications became less accurate when based upon a brief observation and assessment. Study results illustrate this limitation. For example, one bar evolved from one classification type to another since it s original opening. This only became clear following in-depth investigation. Developing a classification system for bars and taverns remains a study strength. Allocating only a brief time to classify a particular bar represents a study limitation.

Finally, the study examines prohibitions against public beer drinking and compares this data to serious crime. The theoretical model allows generalizing punishment for an unrelated minor offense to deterrence of serious crimes. Examining the impact of enforcing only one type of minor offense represents a study weakness. Combining traditional theories to create a more applied and generalized model represents a study strength. The following presentation of ethnographic data illustrates many of these points.

NOTES

[1] The Oklahoma Open Records Act as amended through 1st regular session of 44th Legislature, May 28, 1993. Oklahoma State Statute. Title 51, Section 24A.1-24A.21.

[2] The Oklahoma Municipal League provides lists of similar Oklahoma cities. A service for member cities for comparative analysis.

[3] Crime data is annually published for Oklahoma by The Oklahoma State Bureau of Investigation entitled, Crime in Oklahoma, and for the United States by the United States Department of Justice, through the Federal Bureau of Investigation entitled, Crime in the United States.

[4] Some communities enacted laws with mandatory waiting periods before enforcement. Other community police agencies for example waited ninety days before making arrest or issuing tickets. I contacted and discussed these issues with individual city officials as well as the date of enactment before determining which crime data to include in the before and after enactment categories.

[5] Fraternal organizations for the purpose of this study include the Moose, the Elks, the American Legion, and similar organizations.

CHAPTER 5

Data

Stillwater Ethnography

Stillwater, Oklahoma culture parallels many average size Midwestern American communities. The local chamber of commerce advertises Stillwater s rural quality of life and the culture and the recreational advantages of Oklahoma State University (OSU), one of the State s two major comprehensive universities. Other endorsements include Stillwater s clean environment, low cost of living, easy access to metropolitan cities and growing industrial base. Citizens tend to regard Stillwater as small-town America, a nice place to settle down and raise a family. Most residents accept the myth that Stillwater is virtually crime free, a myth endorsed by local business, industry and government as one of America s 100 safest cities (Franke and Franke, 1984).[1]

Demographically, Stillwater supports a relatively young population; 46.6 percent are between the ages of 18-24.[2] The community, the eighth largest in the State, boasts the fifth largest airport. City government operates with a manager-commission organization providing police, fire, garbage, zoning and ambulance service and a comprehensive city plan available through the year 2020. Eight motor freight companies and Santa Fe rail service service the city. Nine motels provide 832 rooms. Eighty restaurants, 47 churches, 50 social service agencies together with four theaters, 30 lighted tennis courts, 24 city parks and over 5,000 acres of park land are also available. Six museums and three concert halls, the largest seating 1,000, in conjunction with the OSU main campus provide culture and enlightenment to the community. In 1988, the city Parks and Recreation Department received the Outstanding Oklahoma Park Program Award and OSU currently ranks third in the nation in total NCAA athletic championships. Stillwater supports three medical facilities. The largest non-profit hospital contains 145 beds and serves a six county area. The average single-family house costs $62,849. Currently 304 homes are listed with multi-service listing with an average of 236 homes sold annually.[3]

Street Parties

Within the past 25 years, Stillwater, Oklahoma experienced two distinct annual street parties. The first party evolved from the streaking fad that swept college campuses in the early 1970s.[4] In March 1973, the Thursday night before the OSU spring break, several students ran naked along Washington Street, a bar and tavern area adjacent to the OSU campus. By 3:00 a.m. a crowd of over 2,000 students filled the street. Few arrests were made. Police reported excessive underage drinking and watched fires set in trash dumpsters that were then rolled into the street.[5]

By 1978, newspapers and flyers advertised the annual event. That year over 7,000 people filled two city blocks. Police described a drunken crowd. Bars and streets became overcrowded. Police reports included bonfires, broken bottles, streaking, marijuana smoking and a general state of lawlessness. Business owners wet their roofs with garden hoses to prevent fires from pop-bottle rockets that were shot by people in the crowd. Police made 63 arrests for minor alcohol related charges. Later, every person arrested pled guilty. The city reportedly spent $1,000 on police overtime.[6]

The local newspaper reported the 1978 party as, Streakers Night Is Called Success. The paper praised police for asking beer distributors to not sell beer in glass bottles to reduce broken glass. A band paid for by bar owners and the OSU Student Senate played in the street and reportedly focused the mood of the crowd. Hospitals reported no party related injuries. Those business owners previously critical of the event praised city officials for their cooperation and planning.

The most vocal criticism of the party came from Payne County Sheriff Frank Phillips the morning after. The Sheriff complained about the lack of respect the crowd showed for law officers, women and children. When confronted by the Sheriff s statements, one business owner said, If a gathering this large ever again occurs, rest room facilities should be provided. One statement made by the Sheriff was heard. The party cost taxpayers up to $40,000.00 for handling the people arrested and (other) associated costs.

The Stillwater City Manager responded to the Sheriff s comments by forming a committee. The committee ultimately proposed a local ordinance prohibiting the possession and consumption of beer on streets and sidewalks. The ordinance became law by public vote in September 1978. Committee members believed the ordinance would reduce fighting, vandalism and those minor offenses committed by drinkers.

Part of the community agreed with the Sheriff and resented the lawlessness. They wanted the party stopped. Another group of business owners saw the party as good business, but privately admitted the potential for vandalism and violence. Finally, a student group saw the party as a fight for freedom of expression. Each group shared one belief. They all thought that the police were incapable of enforcing a public drinking ban. The ordinance passed before the next annual party.

No one expected almost total voluntary compliance with the new law. Each successive year, the party died a little more. A student group finally rallied 828 signatures in January 1982, and repealed the public drinking ordinance in a referendum election. By then the party was over and could not be resurrected.

A second party began in 1986, almost as spontaneously as the first. At 2:00 a.m., following a Saturday night in late July, 300 students left the eleventh anniversary celebration of a restaurant/bar on another side of the OSU campus. As the bar closed, students blocked the sidewalk and spilled into the street. One hour later, a police sergeant could be seen and heard in the street. The sergeant lectured the bar owner that This is not going to happen again.... This street is not going to be blocked.... There is not going to be another streaker s night in this town as long as I wear this badge....

The spontaneity ended. The following year the bar owner advertised the anniversary celebration. Ads appeared in state and local newspapers. The owner appeared on television talk shows. His face became common and his name a household word. Over 10,000 people attended the next celebration. Area merchants, including restaurants, convenience stores and one clothing store, sold iced beer from livestock watering troughs on city sidewalks. Police responded to 68 party related calls. As a result, 21 people faced arrest on 34 criminal charges. The most serious incident occurred when a drunken person in the crowd drew a loaded and cocked .45 automatic pistol and pointed it at a police officer. Other officers disarmed and arrested the individual. The hospital emergency room treated six minor injuries. Police used 130 hours of officer overtime at a cost of $2,097.50.

Local business hailed the event as an economic windfall. Police reacted to the party by publicizing the arrest information, photographs of the crowd, the cost of the event and the dangers surrounding the armed encounter. Business continued to support the party as an economic necessity. The bar s owner also reacted.

The bar reimbursed the city for the cost of police overtime. The owner announced that sixteen portable toilets would be added to the next celebration. This satisfied citizens complaints of people urinating in yards and on buildings during the party. Civic groups began to support the street party after being promised space for fund raising booths at the next event. The bar hired clowns and street venders. Food distributors planned to serve carnival type foods. The bar even offered the local Boy Scout Troop the opportunity to gather aluminum beer cans from the street following the celebration. Most influential, the bar owner became active in local community affairs.

He joined the Chamber of Commerce. He attended local and state leadership development programs. He began contributing to local causes. His message proclaimed the street party as a family event that was necessary to the economic well being of the community. This message became legitimized in 1991 when the City Visitor and Special Events Board of the Chamber of Commerce commissioned a local professor to study the event.[7]

The professor distributed surveys at motels, restaurants and retail stores throughout the community. The study estimated attendance at the event by counting the number of people who passed a specific point at various times. Three hundred thirty eight surveys indicated that the average day visitor spent $100.00 and the average overnight visitor spent $130.00 during the weekend party. The report concluded that the event contributed $4,714,930.00 to the local economy. By 1993, given larger crowd estimates, the Chamber of Commerce, Visitors and Special Events Bureau estimated that the party generated over $8 million dollars for the community.

My observations differed substantially from the promotion and survey. During the party I saw family type crowds during the early evening. Many couples with children participated in charity games and ate at the food court. In the July heat most participants consumed soft drinks or drank from coolers brought from home. I recognized many in the crowd as local citizens who supported many of the local summertime happenings. After dark, the crowd changed.

With nightfall, the crowd grew younger. Arrest records indicated that the majority of those arrested were college age, from out of town, had no affiliation with OSU and were only in town for the party. Intoxication became the norm. After the party, many participants slept in cars, in yards or in city parks. Police traffic surveys showed that many participants arrived just before the event and brought their own beer, liquor and food. Many in the crowd carried coolers, ice chests and bedrolls. One nearby convenience store closed when the clerks could not control the theft of beer and vandalism to the inside of the business.

By 1993, the event drew over 60,000 participants.[8] That year, over 30 shots were fired in a gang-related shooting seriously injuring one person. A nearby residence burned and fight-related injuries became so frequent that the city began transporting injured people in fire trucks.

As a police administrator, I reacted by first examining the revenue generated by the event. I obtained from the Stillwater Finance Director sales tax reports prepared by the Oklahoma Tax Commission. These reports documented sales taxes collected by Stillwater businesses on a monthly basis. I created then publicized tables and charts illustrating the total sales tax revenue collected during June,

July and August throughout the party s life. This data failed to reflect the $8 million dollar boost in revenue predicted by the research study promoted by the bar owner and subsequently accepted by local business.[9]

Figure 4

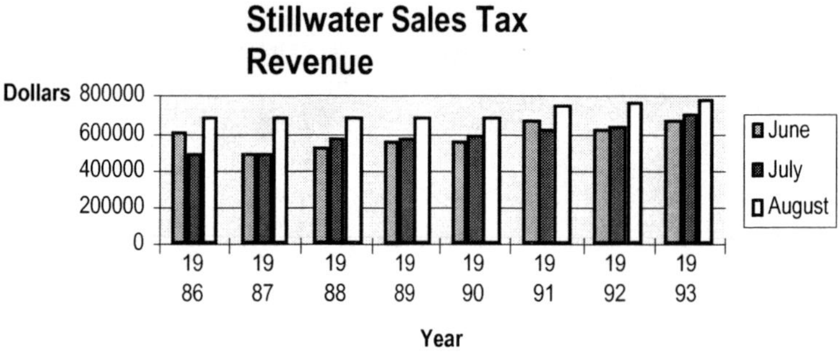

Tax Revenue Data from the Oklahoma Tax Commission from each corresponding year.

Table 2
Stillwater Sales Tax Amounts

Year	June	July	August
1986	$607,278	$495,806	$697,718
1987	492,287	502,581	699,718
1988	525,529	536,605	624,070
1989	568,062	576,983	686,818
1990	560,709	585,862	692,617
1991	669,972	624,592	753,687
1992	627,613	639,886	774,912
1993	679,283	709,739	796,657

Police also publicized the gang-related shooting and the residential arson. Finally, police publicized the cost of hiring 50 off-duty uniformed Tulsa County Sheriff Deputies to augment the 60 Stillwater and 10 OSU Police officers policing the event.

Following the 1993 celebration, the Stillwater City Manager asked the Police Department to study all aspects of the annual street party.[10] Findings, recommendations and an endorsement from the local District Attorney and several church leaders led to re-enacting the public drinking ban by public vote in April 1994.[11]

For the July 1994, celebration businesses advertised a month-long family celebration. Advertising de-emphasized drinking and focused on good food and T-shirt sales. With the public drinking ban in force, fewer than 1,000 people attended the actual night of the annual celebration. Streets remained open. Not a single arrest was made. Many who attended shopped, ate and drank inside the area bars, restaurants and taverns, then spent the night in a local motel. Interestingly, July sales tax revenue increased almost $60,000.00 over the previous year s collection.

Crime Rate Data

As part of the study following the 1993 celebration, I also looked at crime rates. Because Stillwater previously banned public drinking, then four years later repealed the ban, a before, during and after comparison of crime rates became possible. I only considered UCR Part I offenses, those crimes most serious in nature and most likely to become known to police.

The following table reflects Stillwater crime rates and the crime rates from Oklahoma State University and Norman, Oklahoma, the home of Oklahoma University (OU). I chose OSU because OSU is completely surrounded by Stillwater and reports crimes occurring on the university separate from crimes occurring within the city. Also State law and University policy continuously prohibited possession of beer on University property throughout the twelve years that I compared. I selected Norman, Oklahoma because Norman like Stillwater represents a nearby college community and should illustrate any unanticipated cultural issues influencing college students that could affect crime rates. Norman continuously allowed possession and consumption of beer on public streets and sidewalks throughout this same period. Also reported are the crime rates for the entire state of Oklahoma for comparison.

Table 3
Crime Rates Before, During, & After Drinking Ban[12]

	Stillwater	OSU	Norman	Oklahoma
Before:				
1974	35.77	25.36	52.06	40.96
1975	30.65	20.05	60.83	45.78
1976	28.62	21.01	56.46	44.81
1977	26.38	16.29	47.15	41.6
mean	30.355	20.678	54.125	43.288
During:				
1978	23.09	17.01	50.2	41.3
1979	24.88	24.86	53.57	47.03
1980	24.37	23.31	55.48	50.53
1981	26.63	27.99	52.73	48.37
mean	24.743	23.293	52.995	46.808
F-Value:	6.91	0.78	0.13	2034
P-Value:	0.0391	0.4121	0.7306	0.1768
R-Square	0.5354	0.1146	0.0212	0.2808
After:				
1982	35.2	24.45	58.24	52.22
1983	28.12	22.25	54.66	49.29
1984	30.68	24.99	52.05	48.93
1985	33.75	24.45	59.06	54.25
mean	31.938	24.035	56.103	54.173

*Oklahoma crime rates are for the entire State of Oklahoma.
Source, Federal Bureau of Investigation, Uniform Crime Reports, US Government Printing Office, Washington, DC.

From 1974 to 1985, crime gradually increased in the United States (Crime in the United States, 1974-1985). Knowing this, I examined crime rate means the four years before, the four years during and the four years after the Stillwater public drinking prohibition. Crime rates for the State of Oklahoma followed the National trend with average crime rates of 43 before the ban, 47 during the ban and 54 following the Stillwater public drinking ban. OSU less dramatically followed the same trend with crime rates of 21 before the ban, 23 during the ban and 24 following the ban. Norman showed little change with crime rates of 54 before the ban, 53 during the ban and 56 after the Stillwater public drinking ban. The Stillwater data appeared most significant.

Stillwater crime rates averaged 30 before the ban, 25 during the ban and then rose again to 32 following repeal of the public drinking ban. This suggests that at a time when National and State crime rates were increasing, Stillwater serious crime decreased during prohibition of public beer drinking. The data further support the impact of the public drinking prohibition with an increase in Stillwater serious crime to 32 immediately following the repeal of the public drinking ban.

Each of the before, during and after means contained four years of crime rate data. I selected an analysis of variance statistic to compare the variance in the data means. Since most communities that enact local public drinking prohibitions do not usually repeal their laws, before and during data become more useful for comparison.

Analysis of variance results confirmed my subjective observations. Using a confidence level of .05, I found no significant difference in the State of Oklahoma (p=.1768), the OSU (p=.4121) or the Norman (p=.7306) crime rates before and during the Stillwater public drinking ban. I found a significant decrease in serious crime in the Stillwater data during the time of the Stillwater Public beer drinking prohibition (p=.0391).

Table 4
Stillwater Before and During
Crime Rate Analysis of Variance

ANOVA

		Sum of Squares	df	Mean Square	F	Sig.
CRIME	Between Groups	63.000	1	63.000	6.914	.039
	Within Groups	54.671	6	9.112		
	Total	117.671	7			

I analyzed before and during public drinking prohibition data believing that I could locate additional communities with public drinking laws. Still, the Stillwater data remain unique in that it allows for before, during and after comparison. For this reason, I also conducted an analysis of variance of before, during and after the public drinking prohibition. These data support a significant difference in at least one time category (p=.021).

Table 5
Stillwater Before, During, and After
Crime Rate Analysis of Variance

ANOVA

		Sum of Squares	df	Mean Square	F	Sig.
CRIME	Between Groups	114.363	2	57.182	6.072	.021
	Within Groups	84.755	9	9.417		
	Total	199.118	11			

With this information, I conducted a post hoc test to determine which of the variances showed significant differences. I chose Fisher's (1949) Least Significant Difference (LSD) test. The test is less conservative than Duncan or Tukey but is easy to compute and often used with planned comparisons. In this situation, I am dealing with a small amount of data and can subjectively compare before with during crime rates and during with after crime rates. I have less interest in comparing before with after crime rates. Finally, LSD is the default post hoc test on my desktop computer software.[13] I found:

Table 6
Stillwater Crime Rates
Post hoc Test

Multiple Comparisons

Dependent Variable: CRIME
LSD

(I) TIME	(J) TIME	Mean Difference (I-J)	Std. Error	Sig.	95% Confidence Interval	
					Lower Bound	Upper Bound
1.00	2.00	5.6125*	2.170	.029	.7038	10.5212
	3.00	-1.5825	2.170	.484	-6.4912	3.3262
2.00	1.00	-5.6125*	2.170	.029	10.5212	-.7038
	3.00	-7.1950*	2.170	.009	12.1037	-2.2863
3.00	1.00	1.5825	2.170	.484	-3.3262	6.4912
	2.00	7.1950*	2.170	.009	2.2863	12.1037

*. The mean difference is significant at the .05 level.

These data show a statistically significant difference between before and during the public drinking ban (p=.029) and a statistically significant difference between during and after repeal of the drinking prohibition (p=.009). No significant difference is shown between crime rates before and crime rates following repeal of the public drinking ban (p=.484).

I considered, then rejected, a two-way analysis of variance to compare each of the cities listed in Table 7. My experience is that different social forces cause different social groups (cities and universities) to calculate crime rates differently. For example, advertising a safe campus or community can influence patronage in the form of enrollment and new business. Recently, a secretary came to work on a university campus and found that the drawers and cabinets in her office had been rifled. A note on her desk indicated that the door to her office had been found open in the middle of the night by a university police officer. The note asked the secretary to notify police if she discovered anything missing. In this case, the burglary would only be reported if a loss is discovered. Other jurisdictions report the burglary regardless of loss. I chose not to calculate a two-way analysis of variance because different cities calculate crime rates differently. I acknowledge the implied assumption that the same city or university calculates their own crime rates the same over time.

Next, I located twelve communities with public drinking prohibitions similar to Stillwater. County Sheriffs collect crime data for small communities within their jurisdiction. I eliminated one community too small to report individual crime data. I eliminated other communities who did not have at least three years of crime data available before and three years after enacting their local ordinance.[14] This left ten communities available for comparison, including Stillwater.

I then contacted court clerks, crime analysts, public information personnel and police departments for information concerning when police in individual communities actually began enforcing their local law. For example, several communities gave a ninety-day warning period before actually writing tickets on the new law. I then calculated the mean of the three years of crime rates before and the mean of the first three years after enacting public drinking prohibitions. With this information, I compiled the following crime trends.

Table 7

Crime Rates/Trends Before and After Public Drinking Ban

City	Before	After	Difference
Ada	39.83	43.38	3.55
Manhattan	49.58	49.47	**-0.11**
Boulder	74.17	74.11	**-0.06**
Durant	60.36	63.7	3.34
Edmond	45.94	41.57	**-4.37**
Lawton	74.29	61.01	**-13.28**
Jenks	26.85	22.97	**-3.88**
Lawrence	67.55	64.14	**-3.14**
Chico	99.75	81.38	**-18.37**
Stillwater	28.55	24.11	**-4.44**

*Crime Rates are reported in crimes per 1,000 population.

Of the ten communities examined, eight indicated arithmetic decreases in serious crime following enactment of their public drinking prohibition.[15] I wondered if some social force associated with public drinking bans reduced serious crime. Public drinking prohibitions do not ban drinking, only public drinking. I questioned the difference between drinking inside a bar and drinking outside a bar on a street or sidewalk.

The first problem became the variety of types of bars and the various clienteles attracted to individual bar types. Using my classification of bar types, I relied primarily on non-participant observation of ideal-type bars from each category for data.[16] I began observing bars in Stillwater. I then studied bars in Ponca City. Finally, I compared and contrasted these data. The first Stillwater bar is the hotel bar.

Stillwater Hotel Bar

I first saw this particular hotel/motel twenty-seven years ago. The motel was built as a franchise of a major national chain. The lobby and restaurant looked out on parallel rows of two story rooms typical of motel construction in the 1950s. The pool set in an encircled open courtyard. In recent years, the owners added a roof and tiled the courtyard. This enclosed the pool and courtyard and made room for exercise equipment, tables and a small health center. The formal bar sat almost hidden behind the restaurant and opened into the now enclosed pool and recreation area. Real and plastic tropical plants in large clay pots further hid the bar from the family-type atmosphere promoted in the courtyard area.

The motel is of average size for the community and seems to attract upper middle class clientele.[17] Most guests consisted of families on vacation, business people or small convention type activities. The well-paid pipeline, oil field or wheat harvest laborer would likely feel out of place. Conventioneers or alumni with tickets to a local university-sporting event would feel at home.

As I drove into the parking lot on my first night of research, the area seemed quiet. The marquee welcomed the 25th anniversary of the local high school class of 1972. The heat and humidity of late June hung heavy in the dark and partly overcast 10:00 p.m. sky. I stood for a moment alone in the dark parking lot. I looked around and laughed to my self.

OSU began as Oklahoma A&M, the State agriculture school. Even in 1971 when I first enrolled as an incoming freshman, OSU was nationally recognized for research in agriculture and livestock. In 1971, this particular hotel neighbored both the city limits and a large red native stone barn boasting a whitewashed sign reading SWINE. That night, the barn and the welded wire barnyard fences enclosed what residents not so affectionately referred to as the hog farm. Newer businesses neighbors in the area included two convenience stores, a restaurant and other small stores. Business marquees frequently referenced the hog farm and the always-present smell. The hot and humid summer night exaggerated the smell. It was my first night of research; I went inside.

Activity bustled around the jacuzzi and the indoor pool just outside the bar. Middle-aged adults drank from a variety of alcoholic beverages.[18] Cigars seemed to be the smoke of choice for both men and women. The small crowd seemed reminiscent of people from a busy day who were not wanting to let it end. Although most everyone drank, states of intoxication appeared inconsistent.

Just as a table of people started getting loud, something seemed to quickly calm them. When this happened it seemed closely associated with the presence of a large group of preadolescent children playing in the pool and roaming around the courtyard. I sensed, then found, the presence of inconspicuous parents throughout the area. Middle-aged couples sat quietly outside their rooms, walked along the courtyard sidewalks or sat quietly in the shadows around the pool and jacuzzi. Those who drank seemed keenly aware of these parents and the family environment. The whole setting seemed to say that things were not to get too far out of hand.

The actual bar hid behind a door warning those under 21 years of age to stay out. Both real and plastic plants hid the entrance from those not looking for the bar. Inside, a long highly polished wooden bar supported about twenty padded bar stools. The bar smelled of a fresh coat of polyurethane that somehow matched the simulated-leather vinyl on the chairs and stools. Another ten tables, each with four chairs, sat on deep piled carpet that looked like it could never really be cleaned. Ten additional taller tables each with two bar-type stools lined the walls. A baseball game played on a small television mounted near the ceiling; no one seemed interested. A portable disk jockey sound system looked permanently installed next to a dance floor barely large enough to hold the three couples who were dancing the twist. In all, the bar contained fifteen customers.

As I sat down at the bar, the bartender studied my presence the way a salesperson sizes up a customer. I ordered a soft drink. Sitting next to me, a single over-dressed man about 40 years old wearing a straw fedora-style hat, tie and two-tone shoes ordered bourbon and water. He said that he was in town on business. His nervousness and the way he constantly looked around said that he sensed the lack of action. He finished one drink and left. Next to him a 60-year-old man sat with what appeared to be his 30 year old son or grandson. The man told the bartender that they were traveling on business. The relationship between this man and his companion took on the air of a right of passage type pilgrimage prior to dad turning over the business. One couple played pool on the only pool table. They both wore new well-pressed western clothing. The man s clothing seemed to be holding in the evidence of encroaching middle age. One table of people, the dancers, wore nametags from the high school reunion. This left one couple at the end of the bar and another couple playing darts.

The man at the end of the bar appeared about 25 to 30. He looked Hispanic with black hair nearly reaching his shoulders. His dark searching eyes accentuated both a quiet and mild demeanor. His washed hands failed to hide the stains and calluses from hard work. He sipped from a soft drink as he watched the crowd and the woman sitting next to him. He wore a light colored shirt and modest trousers that looked both recently pressed and well worn. He and the woman beside him made an unusual couple.

The woman looked about 35. She drank about one beer per hour, an amount inconsistent with the high level of intoxication that she exhibited. Her low-cut, high-cropped red blouse exposed both her brassier and her stomach. She also wore cut-off jeans with real rather than designer patches. I never saw her shoes as she danced bare footed for each customer individually in the bar. Her short black hair looked bleached red from the sun and uneven as though she had trouble cutting the back. Her tanned and lined face revealed mileage beyond her years. Finally, her legs looked weathered and scratched as though from working in the Oklahoma green-briar and thorn-weed.

As the bartender brought my drink, she yelled across the bar I m buying his drink. The bartender leaned across the bar and quietly told me not to worry that she comes in about once every month and buys everyone their first drink. When the bartender charged her for a soft drink, she danced over to talk to me.

She told me that her 89 year old husband has an 80 acre pig farm about 20 miles east of town. As she became more comfortable, the farm shrunk to 60, then 40 acres. Once a month, the hired hand, she called him her companion, brings her to town for a good time. It seemed important for her to tell me that her companion had his own room, didn t drink and was there to take care of her. She told me about her seventh grade education almost as though it made her seem more vulnerable, almost flirtatious. The companion watched emotionless as though he had seen the scene before and was sure of its ending. As the bartender approached, the woman returned to her companion who was still sitting at the other end of the bar.

The bartender continued to study me as I talked to the woman. As he brought me a napkin, he spoke apologetically about the woman while confirming her story. Once a month the woman comes in, gets drunk, buys drinks and gets a room with her friend. The friend doesn t drink but quietly watches and takes care of her. The bartender lost interest in me after I failed to express annoyance with the situation. Later in the evening, I repeatedly watched the same scenario play out involving the bartender, the woman and each new customer. I left without asking if her monthly visits corresponded to her husband s income, social security benefit or other retirement or assistance checks.

The final couple in the bar seemed unremarkable at first. Their relationship appeared tastefully flirtatious like a middle-aged recently married couple or reunited high school sweethearts. The man wore a reunion nametag. He seemed a little more casually dressed than the rest of the reunion and definitely more at home in the bar. The woman dressed slightly younger than her age. She wore a vest-type blouse that revealed a black lace camisole on each pool shot. She wore black satin slacks that covered her flat shoes making her shorter than any man present. It was her long straight blond hair that looked more at home on a college coed than one of the reunion participants. Neither person wore a wedding ring.

The blond-haired woman ritualistically reappeared each time I visited the bar. About 8:00 p.m. the woman stopped by, looked in the bar, and left. By ten she returned, knowing who had been in the bar since eight, and their level of intoxication. First she placed three quarters on the pool table. Later when no one was looking she reached under the rail and released the balls without paying. She studied the pool balls like she studied the crowd. Soon she was playing pool, darts or dancing with someone from the bar.

Neither the bartender nor the waitress acknowledged her by name but their behavior seemed to facilitate her presence. For example, the waitress asked everyone in the bar for their drink order except this woman. For this woman, the waitress turned to the man next to her and asked will you be ordering for the lady. The bartender seemed to know without asking which drink order belonged to this particular woman. He mixed her drinks without liquor. Once when a drink spilled on the bar, this woman knowingly reached under the bar for an out-of-sight towel. Finally, I watched the woman leave the bar with a different gentleman each night. My research failed to obtain additional information about this particular woman, her occupation or her reason for being in the hotel bar.

Repeated visits to the same hotel bar clarified many of my first observations. No one drank in the parking lot or on the outside property other than to carry a drink to or from a car.[19] On nights when business was slow or nights without an organized group at the hotel, the bar closed. A uniformed security guard sometimes walked through the bar, but the bartender controlled the atmosphere and the crowd. The bartender watched each new customer and assessed his or her acceptance of activity in the bar. When an intoxicated person offended a customer, the bartender would find someone to take the intoxicated person to his or her room. When no one complained or when customers seemed amused by drunken behavior, the bartender both continued to sell drinks and allowed the activity to continue. All seemed fine as long as the customers were happy.

Evidence of the bartender s control became most apparent during a small fight. One Saturday night, the family remnants of a wedding party celebrated until after 1:00 a.m. A fight started when one woman told another woman that the second woman s husband fathered the first woman s second child. The fight consisted of hair pulling, scratching, torn clothes and overturned tables and chairs. Two male family members finally pulled the two women apart as the bartender arrived at the fight.

The bartender immediately ordered the waitress to turn up the lights. He then turned to both of the fighting women and the men holding them and ordered them out after I (the bartender) finish some bookkeeping. The older of the two men protested. The bartender negotiated allowing one woman to take a short walk, outside. The bartender then bought the other woman a drink on the house. When the first woman returned, the bartender also bought her a drink. The bookkeeping comment became apparent as the bar began to close. The second woman was responsible for the $200.00 bar tab for the entire wedding party.

Things seemed different outside the bar in the courtyard. Even though the law saw the courtyard as a licensed extension of the bar, the atmosphere seemed more like a public park or recreation area. In the courtyard people seemed constrained by families watching their young children swim and play on the recreation equipment. The uniformed security guard spent more time in the courtyard. I never saw the security guard take an official action. The guard looked neat and well polished in his appearance. His quiet almost timid presentation made him seem incapable of any official action. When behavior approached something inappropriate, looks and the perceived threats of censure from families in the area took care of the problem. On one occasion, one woman became very loud and intoxicated. As other adults and children in the courtyard began to stare, two men from the woman s table helped walk her to a room.

Anxieties sometimes rose around 2:00 a.m. At 2:00 a.m., the formal bar closed and forced those drinkers from the bar out into the common area. The deadline came for deciding who was leaving with whom and where they were going. Acquaintances made in the bar helped to mediate minor conflicts. Friends also took friends with them almost like designated guardians. During this time, the presence of the uniformed guard seemed to settle disagreements. Again, I saw no official action from the security guard other than his official presence.

Stillwater Neighborhood Bar

The weather seemed uncharacteristically cool for the July night that I first visited the neighborhood bar. The bar resided in an older almost downtown part of the city. The bar lacked real parking causing customers to park along the deserted street in front of businesses well past their closing time. Over the years, I had forgotten about the bar.

It blended into the local landscape. Residents pass by seldom taking notice. This suddenly changed as I stepped inside and memories rushed back.

In the early 1980s, a couple of drifters came through town. The woman of the pair ended up in this bar. She met and drank with a local man inside the bar before enticing him out the back door where the male drifter waited. The pair attacked the man with a baseball bat. The beating left the victim s head unrecognizable. As the victim died, the pair robbed his body taking his wallet and keys. With these, they found his address and burglarized his home. Later a tabloid-type detective magazine publicized the ball bat murder, arrest and trial.

Because of the murder and publicity, the bar gained a reputation as a rough place. I remembered it differently. The few reports of minor disturbances over the last fifteen years were always well over before the police arrived. My experiences were that people inside the bar took care of themselves. Like arriving at many minor family disturbances, the people did not want involvement from the police or anyone else.

Inside, the bar looked bigger than I remembered. As I walked around, I found that the back storage room now contained a pool table. The wall between the bar and the business next door had been broken out. The doorway appeared clean of debris but looked as though a truck had driven through a rock wall. This provided room for another pool table and an electronic dartboard. An electronic poker machine sat on one end of the bar.[20] Both the electronic dartboard and poker machine looked strangely out of place. Dust covered the black and white portable television that sat atop the jukebox; it played without sound. The jukebox offered the only opportunity for music. Throughout the evening, the jukebox seldom played.

Neon signs, from their first wave of popularity, frequented the walls. Many of the original ceiling fans missed one or more blades. Plastic stand-up fans wearing their Wal-Mart price tags circulated stale air. The floor missed many of the one-inch, six sided ceramic floor tiles common in drugstores and bathrooms in the 1920s. This left the small diner-type tables with broken Formica tops sitting unsteady on the uneven floor.

The chairs looked secondhand and matched neither their tables nor themselves. A few restaurant type booths filled the corners.

Each exposed stained foam rubber through tears in black vinyl. My soft drink came in the can and people casually drank beer form bottles rather than glasses.[21] I felt overdressed wearing clean clothes.

At forty-four I was easily the youngest of the nine people in the bar. The woman bartender seemed at ease and at home. She wore pink polyester stretch pants with elastic topped fuzzy slippers. She took little particular interest in anyone in the place, including me. The only person that I recognized by name was the stereotypical town drunk at the end of the bar. He displayed an extremely high yet comfortable state of intoxication. He slowly drank and enjoyed a quiet conversation with the bartender. Around midnight, he slowly made his way out the back door almost as if he could no longer handle the late night hours. He neither recognized me nor acknowledged my presence.

The two women in the bar wore loose white cotton tops with one too many buttons left undone and tight jeans. The women seemed attached to two particular men. Everyone accepted this arrangement. The bar lacked the bantering and flirtation often present in mixed groups. Everyone seemed at home without a well-defined agenda. Roles and territories were long ago established and not contested. No one moved around. It was almost as though each person had their own place to sit, their own pool cue and their own topic of conversation. In three hours, not more than twelve drinks were sold.

At 1:00 a.m. the bartender reached from under the counter for a small plastic bucket. She made her rounds to each pool table. She turned off the cracked plastic beer advertisement light above each table then unlocked the change box. She emptied the change into the bucket and left the lock laying open on the floor as if to keep any late-night burglar from prying it free. When she finished, the five pool tables yielded less than a hand full of quarters. She took four of these quarters to the jukebox and started the music.

When the music started, the only remaining customers, a man and a woman, left their pool game. The couple called the bartender by name and politely asked if they could order two more beers. The bartender got the beer, took their money, turned on the house lights, picked up a Master padlock and looked at me. I asked if it was time to go; it was thirty minutes before the legal closing time. She nodded yes without saying a word. I heard the pad lock being placed on the hasp as I walked from the bar. I left the bar, but returned shortly after the 2:00 a.m. legal closing time.

The two remaining cars that were parked outside were gone. The bar looked dark and quiet. As I drove down the back alley, I saw the town drunk again. A piece of cardboard covered a discarded easy-chair seat cushion from behind a nearby furniture store. The man had pulled the cushion under some nearby shrubs. It looked as though he had passed out on the cushion just out of sight of the casual observer. Even though I drove right past him, he did not move. Interestingly, he was lying on his stomach with his head turned downhill and to the side. This seemed to be an almost instinctive position to keep from aspirating should he get sick in his unconscious condition. The following morning, the man was gone and the seat cushion had been returned to the discarded easy chair still sitting behind the furniture store.

Repeated visits to the neighborhood bar yielded similar observations. Saturday nights sometimes drew fifteen or more customers. Intoxication levels sometimes seemed high; drunkenness always seemed low. Even highly intoxicated persons seemed to take care of themselves. Although people sometimes remained for hours without talking, everyone knew everyone s name and seemingly knew quite a bit about each other. People talked about the mundane routines of their lives. No one disagreed. No one fought. For many the bar seemed to be a home away from home, a place to go to log the leftover hours at the end of the day.

Stillwater Restaurant Bar

I first walked into the restaurant bar on a Saturday night in late July. The bar had opened about two years earlier with an influx of national bar and restaurant chains. The owners built the building from the ground up in an outlying business districts cluttered with strip malls, fast food and chain stores. I later learned that the bar represented an international franchise of bar and grills. The bartender actually bragged that the chain constructs every bar on the same floor plans. Some are bigger than others, but if you walk into one in another country, they all look the same you feel right at home .

The entire restaurant seemed to encircle the sunken bar located in the center of the establishment. The restaurant reflected a sporting decor. Replicas of antique fishing, hunting and a variety of sports memorabilia decorated the walls. Upon close inspection, many of the duck decoys and the other decorations were molded plastic. Televisions played without sound throughout the restaurant. Recorded music on one occasion and music from a local popular radio station on others, filled the air.

As I entered the bar, a hostess near the door laid down a telephone, greeted me and directed me to a table near the bar. In all, four people sat at the bar. Another thirty-five customers ate in small groups at tables. The tables surrounded the central sunken bar that appeared accentuated with indirect lighting and polished brass. The sporting theme and the tables and chairs surrounding the central sunken bar resembled an ancient coliseum causing subconscious excitement.

With the exception of one couple at the bar that looked like they were on their first date, everyone ate. The menu contained a variety beyond that of the local diner. For most middle class families, the selections held unfamiliar names. I found the portions less than generous and the prices within reach for a special occasion. Families ate with small children. Teenagers sat next to middle age couples and senior citizens.

The age of customers varied as greatly as the food. Employees working the bar appeared to be in their early 20s. The reason for being at the bar was to eat. In repeated visits, even those who sat at the bar ordered food.

The behavior of the restaurant employees best describes the culture of the establishment. Although the franchise was locally owned, employees enjoyed the benefits of the national chain. Supervisors, for example, participated in the company management development program with opportunities to transfer to larger bars in larger markets. Other employees also enjoyed the benefits and privileges of a large business. The bartender provided this information; employee behavior supported it.

Each visit there seemed to be more employees in the restaurant than customers. Not a single employee looked over 30 years old. On repeated visits, the hostess frequently returned to his/her personal telephone conversation at the greeting station after seating me. At two other workstations, waitresses frequently chatted casually on telephones. When employees were not on the telephone, they stood in small groups and talked. Almost on cue an employee would leave the group, hurriedly wipe down a section of tables and chairs or refill condiment dispensers, then return to the conversation. After a table of customers left, another employee would leave the group, hurriedly clean the table, and return. Individuals took turns on the three available telephones. Noticing on one occasion that I had waited over ten minutes without being served, the bartender gave me my soft drink on the house. This provided the opportunity for conversation.

The bartender explained the large number of employees as leftovers from the dinning hour. Employees were guaranteed an eight-hour shift by company policy. I made three weekend visits to the restaurant bar. Just as each restaurant in the chain resembles the other, each of my visits reflected other visits. Sometimes the restaurant was busy, sometimes not. Customers and many of the employees were different between visits, but the type of employees and the type of customers remained the same. The bartender once pointed out that he had a couple of regulars at the bar. These turned out to be three college students in their early twenties.

The female students ordered finger-food appetizers with their beer. Although they flirted with the bartender, their interests seemed to be to have a light meal before a night of partying. Both their appearance and the casual way they drank indicated an age in their early 20s, but conformably above the 21 year old drinking age. Their easy interaction in the restaurant and their designer clothing indicated upper-middle class. The women finished their food. The flirtation ended. The women left.

As the bartender talked and the night grew later, employees would individually walk behind the bar, pour a shot of liquor in a glass and disappear into a back portion of the business. Near closing time, the number of employees in the front business area began to dwindle.

The noise from the back increased. As I left to look for the restroom, I found a large table of employees. Many looked like kitchen workers and under the legal drinking age. Shot glasses covered the table. The bartender explained this behavior by saying they re getting a head start on Saturday night. The restaurant closed at midnight, two hours before the mandated legal closing time. As the restaurant closed, otherwise lethargic employees almost ran from the building. Conversations and accelerating vehicles indicated that employees left with an excitement that their evening had just begun.

Stillwater Theme Bar

The theme bar resided in an older light business district of the city adjacent to the University. I first visited the building in 1971. Then it was a diner run by two unmarried sisters. They lived upstairs and were seldom seen outside the building. The diner served lunch and supper. Lunch cost 65 cents, supper $1.25. As you entered, you received a plate at the door with a piece of meat. Glasses and silverware were available as you proceeded to bench style wooden picnic-type tables. Large well-worn sweat-covered aluminum pitchers held iced tea. Similar aluminum bowls held vegetables and huge fresh baked rolls, obviously made from scratch. Aside from the meat, it was all you could eat. In the mid 1980s the sisters sold the building and disappeared.

The building became a small bar. At first, it sold beer. Later the business expanded to offer liquor and beer. With more recent changes in State law, the bar also became a restaurant selling food, T-shirts and other souvenirs. Because of the bars legal status as a restaurant, people under 21 years of age were admitted.[22] For this reason the bar s popularity grew. Over the years trendy remodeling changed both the inside and outside of the building. One thing didn t change. The theme of the bar remained its appeal to OSU, OSU students and more recently OSU alumni.

At the time of my research, the original 1930s rock exterior enclosed the modern trendy bar inside. Stained oak planking made up the stairs, banisters and railings. Antique metal signs advertising everything from Dr. Pepper to five-cent cigars decorated the walls. Laminated oak tables under multiple layers of polyurethane accentuated matching chairs, booths and barstools. The high-tech sound system supported continuous digital sound or live bands. The antique style metal light fixtures with central rheostat control matched throughout the bar. As I walked in the door, both the atmosphere and the crowd mirrored the decor.

My first research visit came on a Saturday night in mid July. The University summer session was well under way but still left the community (and the bar) void of the larger number of fall and spring semester students. As I walked in the door, the assistant manager in charge of doormen/bouncers greeted me.

The doorman, an undergraduate sociology student said that his professor had told him that I was studying bars. He wanted to show off an observation that he learned from working in the bar. The doorman/student walked over and turned a dial that lowered the lights. Instantly the intensity of the conversation throughout the bar increased. After a few minutes he slowly turned the lights back up. The volume of the conversation again returned to its original level. Before the night was over, each of the bar s various older managers knew of my presence and stopped by my table to visit.[23] Otherwise, I seemed invisible to employees and customers.

The doorman estimated about 150 customers in the two story, multi-room bar. Entering the bar resembled the well-rehearsed, well-structured bureaucracy indicative of the business. Regular customers and those obviously over 21 years old immediately passed through the door. For the regulars, this held that same prestige of a waitress asking if you will have the usual. For others, entry became a short line and an identification (ID) check for age. This process and the air of familiarity with which people walked in the door helped make the regular customers stand out. Regulars also knew the price of drinks and the location of pool cues and bathrooms. Regulars seemed to be served more quickly at the bar and were somewhat more likely to be alone than with a group.

I walked up to the bar and ordered a soft drink. After offering to pay, the bartender said no charge on soft drinks, it s our designated driver program. I confessed to not being a designated driver; it did not matter. The glass, crushed ice, and swizzle stick made my soft drink indistinguishable from the mixed drinks carried by others. I felt very comfortable walking around the bar or standing and watching pool games. I watched a few people dance and I pretended to listen to the music. It was as though I was invisible as I listened to conversations between people in the bar.

Eclectic describes the regular bar clientele. The first regular customer that I identified was a woman in her early 20s. Noticing me watching her, another customer told me that she worked in a bank, was recently divorced, had no interest in men and was well on her way to becoming a drunk. I lost track of the number of imported beers that she drank as she played pool with whoever was convenient. At last call, she settled her bar tab and left alone. I do not believe that she spoke over a dozen words to her various pool companions the entire evening. From her interaction with the crowd, she seemed to just want to get through the night.

I identified two women sitting at the bar as regulars. They looked to be in their late 30s. They wore designer clothes, make-up and expensive jewelry complete with wedding rings. Their dresses seemed short for their age but accentuated the comfortable manner in which they controlled their exaggerated high-heeled shoes. They sat quietly, often not even talking to each other, until approached by two or more men. Then they became almost overly flirtatious, accepting drinks, dancing and seeming to hold on to the conversation even when the men seemed ready to move on. Toward the end of the evening, the two women seemed to sparkle as they repeatedly rebuffed offers of rides from men. The two women left together. They left laughing as though they had thoroughly enjoyed their evening. It seemed as though the evening provided a safe reassurance of their youth and desirability.

Another regular identified himself as a university professor. His small stature, white hair and long white beard made estimating his age difficult. He drank a number of mixed drinks but never lost a dignity that seemed important to him. As he noticed people that he knew he seemed to go out of his way to be friendly. It almost seemed that he wanted those that he met to know that he was a real person away from his professional responsibilities, just like them.

Finally, the last group of regulars arrived late. These were employees of other branches of the same theme bar. This young mixed group generally drank beer and shots of liquor as though they needed to catch up with the intoxication level of the rest of the crowd. As I watched, I learned that their arrival amounted to their weekend ritual. They came to this bar after the bar that they work in closed. Because they were employees, they drank at a discount. This also provided the opportunity to socially network with higher status bosses within the bar s company structure.

I also identified a number of newcomers. The first consisted of a group of six men from a nearby small town celebrating their company s softball championship. They drank beer, mixed drinks and straight liquor shots. After two hours of drinking and singing to the music, bouncers ejected them. This followed an earlier warning for pouring beer on downstairs customers from an upstairs balcony. Bouncers finally asked them to leave after they poured liquor from their shots onto bar table and set it afire to see if the liquor would burn. The ejection was swift, sure and left the unmistakable impression that it would become physical given half a chance. It did not.

Most newcomers came in small groups, usually two men or two women. The pairs of men or women either sat at tables or walked around the bar. Everyone drank. Those younger men who sat at tables seemed alert to everyone in the bar. They appeared to be in the right place to be seen and they wanted to be noticed. On one occasion, two men watched two other older men standing and visiting throughout the bar. The seated men watched these older men intently for over ten minutes until their eyes met and the seated men achieved the opportunity to wave.

Men and women in their 30s who walked around seemed almost like hosts and hostesses. They greeted people that they knew, smiled and nodded to people that they thought that they knew. They struck up conversations with people that they wanted to know.

The bar clearly possessed a well-advertised theme. It catered to the college culture. Those inside wanted to associate with that theme or others drawn by that theme. On an individual level, other social forces worked. For some the agenda was to be seen in a popular trendy place. For some the agenda was to meet someone for sexual or romantic purposes. For some it was the personal reassurance that they remained attractive and desirable. For some it was that they were still capable of childish foolishness. For each their presence inside the bar held importance.

The theme bar also drew crowds outside in the parking area adjacent to the bar. Here, emotions rather than well-defined agendas ruled. The outside group included a large number of young people. These people were too young to get inside, but old enough to want to be seen at a popular bar. In the past I observed college age entrepreneurs selling beer from ice chests out of the beds of pickup trucks at inflated prices to these youths. I also identified out of town gang recruiters and known drug dealers visiting with these youths. I saw neither activity on my chosen nights of research. I did see others.

The softball players remained outside after being ejected. They displayed anger and resentment at being thrown out, but refused to leave the area. The outside group also contained those individuals too intoxicated to get inside. Frequent topics of conversation surrounded the negative aspects of being too young, too drunk or too disruptive to get inside. Criticisms of laws concerning public intoxication, drinking age and public drinking, frequented conversations. This led to criticisms of bouncers, doormen and police.

Interestingly when a police car did drive by, the outside crowd took little notice. The officer in his/her air-conditioned car with the windows up seemed well insulated and far removed, as s/he looked straight down the street. Sensing this distance from the police seemed to intensify those critical of the police and authority figures. Those who did express the same attitudes and behavior of inside customers seemed to be headed inside or away from the area. Those ejected and those who could not get in, set the mood for the crowd outside. Clearly, the various individual agendas present inside faded to negative pessimistic discussions in the back parking lot.

Ponca City Ethnography

Ponca City (Ponca) lies 45 minutes north of Stillwater by car and parallels Stillwater in many ways. Most local businesses and the Chamber of Commerce promote Ponca on a historical theme. The story involves the creation of the town. An Arkansas entrepreneur, B. S. Barnes, located the current Ponca City town-site in 1893, prior to the opening of the Cherokee Strip Land Run. Barnes surveyed the area, platted a town-site and sold holding certificates for $2.00 each. Following the opening of the Territory, Barnes drew lots to locate certificate holders with the location of their individual pieces of land. In essence, the community began with an illegal lottery.

This theme continued as Ponca advertised itself as where the 20s still roar. At the time of my visits, the theme focused on the growth of the City during the oil boom of the 1920s. Residents intended this theme to draw business to the local industrial site and the local homes of past millionaires. In recent years, the City purchased many of these homes that had been converted to hotels and convention centers.

Demographically, Ponca City contained 12,294 families or a total population of about 26,359 people.[24] The largest group, 27 percent, were between the ages of 18-34. Culturally, Stillwater contained three percent Black and six percent Asian, a result of the University influence. Ponca contained three percent Black and six percent Native American, a result of the nearby Ponca Indian Tribe. Otherwise, Ponca generally paralleled the demographics of the State of Oklahoma with one exception.

Ponca City was a company town. Conoco Petroleum employeed 2,500 people. The next largest single employer, the local school system, employed 850. Tongue-in-cheek comments at business and professional conferences include, What s good for Conoco is good for Ponca. And, I buy Conoco gas, you never know who s watching. Indicators also appeared throughout the city in the form of logos on clothing, sponsorship of little league teams and plaques commemorating civic contributions.

Ponca City operated a municipal airport with a single 6,200-foot instrument approved runway capable of supporting the largest corporate jets. The field provided daily commuter flights to Oklahoma City and Dallas. The average single-family home sold for $79,800; at the time 80% of the available homes were occupied. The average home was listed 69 days before sale. Higher education was located 14 miles west of town at Tonkawa Junior College or Oklahoma State University in Stillwater. Educationally, Ponca secondary students ranked one-half point below the National average in ACT scores, but one point above the State average of 20.3. Ponca maintained 50 physicians, 20 dentists, 10 pharmacies, and four medical facilities.

The Ponca City Economic Development Foundation summarized the community with, From rodeos to research labs, from education to health care, from spectator sports to economic opportunities, from culture to commerce, from science to art . The demography showed a moderate size Midwestern community. The people emphasized growth and community leaders publicized plans for continued growth and development. For Ponca City this growth is planned to be in the form of business, small convention facilities and tourism.

Ponca City Hotel Bar

I selected this hotel bar for a number of reasons. The bar faced the main thoroughfare through town and was franchised by the same chain as the hotel bar studied in Stillwater. The area contained a number of independently owned businesses. For example, a muffler shop, an ice cream store and a grocery store neighbor the bar from across the street. Behind the bar began 1950s style residential neighborhoods with wooden frame houses and single car garages. I found both similarities and differences from the same-type Stillwater bar.

My first visit came on a Friday night in late May. The evening still held the radiant energy of the hot summer day together with a futile hope for rain. The parking lot seemed full of middle class type cars and pickup trucks with in-state tags. Otherwise the street, the parking lot and the city seemed quiet. The bar looked more like an add-on rather than part of the original hotel. The local hotel began in the mid 1960s as a single building. A pool was later constructed outside adjacent to a maintenance building and Laundromat. Half dozen children either swam or talked quietly around the pool. Like the Stillwater hotel, the Ponca hotel appeared clean and well maintained. Unlike the Stillwater hotel, the Ponca hotel showed little evidence of remodeling other than the add-on bar. I heard music as I approached the door. The bar itself held surprises.

I entered an unexpectedly large bar with nearly 100 customers by the end of the evening. A 40-foot bar supported two bartenders with both room and business for more. The bartenders never slowed. After paying a two-dollar cover charge, I walked past four, six-to-eight person restaurant-style booths that separated one end of the disco-type dance floor. Mirrors covered a wall at the back of the dance area. A raised platform with tables and chairs completed the dancing enclosure. A deejay took requests from an open booth built to connect the bar with the dance floor.

The music ranged from hard rock to country and everything else in between. Thirty bar stools lined the bar. In addition to four built-in televisions, seventeen neon signs all promoting a different brand of beer decorated the top of the bar. Tables with either two or four chairs covered most of the remaining floor space.

The type of corrugated tin found on rural barns covered one wall. Saddles, tack, boots and branding irons covered one wall. Mounted elk, big horn sheep, mule deer and moose heads also hung from the walls. One interesting decoration hung directly over the bar. The mount consisted of a moose head with elk antlers. The moose wore a Budweiser ball cap and a scarf around it s neck; no one else seemed to either notice or care. I sat down and ordered coffee. All coffee and soft drinks were on the house. Wearing a knit shirt, denim blue jeans and boots, I blended in.

As I looked around, the bar represented everything and everyone. One man in his early 30s wore a business suit and sat at a table with two women in their early 20s wearing cut-off jeans and tank-top shirts. Customers ranged from late teens to upper 60s. The door person failed to check the age of even the youngest customers entering the bar. Bartenders and waiters failed to check age when serving drinks. Yet, no one in the diverse crowd appeared overly intoxicated. Footwear further illustrates the diversity of the group. Men and women, young and old, wore sandals, designer tennis shoes, polished dress shoes and cowboy boots. Women wore party dresses, jeans and overalls. Some women wore high-heels. Waitresses wore a uniform of T-shirts, shorts and combat or hunting style boots. Interestingly the diversity of individual agendas mirrored the diversity of the crowd.

Patrons discussed work, school, families and each other. A few individuals obviously looked for companionship; most looked only for a good time. The bar catered to not only business from the hotel, but also to local young and middle class clientele. One of the most interesting aspects of the bar were those formal social controls intended to control the crowd.

I paid a cover charge to a woman at a booth near the door each evening that I visited the bar. A man sat behind the booth wearing a T-shirt with the word SECURITY printed boldly across the front and back. The bartenders wore the same shirts. In addition to the waitresses, three men bussed tables and served drinks. These men wore the same security shirt. I never witnessed any trouble in the bar. At closing the men wearing the security shirts followed the customers out the door. Customers left seemingly with a destination in mind. No one lingered in the parking lot or around the area. Few customers left for the hotel.

Marked police cars occasionally drove by, but the officers seemed not to notice the crowd and never stopped. Other than their presence and the SECURITY T-shirts, I saw no official action on the part of the advertised security personnel.

I first placed the bar within the category of the hotel bar. I later discovered someone not associated with the hotel locally owned the bar. Further, the contract with the hotel for space differed from the contract with the hotel in Stillwater.[25] These differences also influence the motivation for profit and behavior within the bar.

Those hotel guest customers within the bar quickly became absorbed into the eclectic discussions of other customers. Both customers and employees immediately, when asked, describe the bar as the best in town. I found the bar to possess many of the descriptive qualities and social controls of the theme bar. The good time/party atmosphere best describes the theme of this bar.

Ponca City Neighborhood Bar

I left the bar early on my first visit to the Ponca neighborhood bar. It was early June. The hot Oklahoma summer seemed inevitable and unrelenting. For blue—collar workers it meant hot nightsafter hot days with short tempers and little to do. I began my evening by driving and walking around the neighborhood of the neighborhood bar.

The neighborhood was located about a mile northeast of the petroleum refinery, the cities largest employer. With the predominately southwest wind, the neighborhood escaped the smell of oil and what the local people call sour gas. The neighborhood contained much of the oldest housing within walking distance of the blue-collar refinery jobs. The WPA sidewalks long ago succumbed to the roots of oak and elm shade trees. A thin coat of asphalt on the street had long ago worn away exposing paving bricks. The houses were mostly white wood-frame built on natural rock foundations and what appeared to be the same floor plan. Tract housing failed to adequately explain the physical closeness or similarity of the late 1940s style homes. Many people lounged on front porches in spite of the upper 90-degree evening temperatures. Others planted flowers or worked in backyard vegetable gardens.

A few window air conditioners groaned. Mostly it was silent. Many of the houses wore fresh paint. The lawns looked and smelled of fresh mowing. Well-maintained cars ranging from new to vintage, hid in one-car garages. Streets lacked the expected junk cars found in adjacent run-down areas nearer the single set of railroad tracks which ran through town. Many of the backyards held old aluminum flat—bottomfishing boats, the kind that you throw in the back of a pickup or tie on top of a car. The boats held fishing poles and tackle indicative of recent use. People in the area wore jeans or khaki work pants and undershirts. Hispanic and Native American cultures seemed equally represented with White.

As I first drove and later walked through the neighborhoods surrounding the neighborhood bar, I began to identify the culture of individual homes. A Hispanic family lived immediately south of the bar. The father typically worked outside around the house until just before dark. He always wore light colored loosely fitting trousers and either an unbuttoned shirt or an undershirt, the knit kind without a collar or sleeves. Latin music came from an open window on evenings that his wife worked in the front yard flower garden. The man spoke Spanish with his wife. Spanish and English seemed to mix as the couple spoke to their teen-age children who never seemed to have time to listen.

A Native American family lived across the street. With the front door open, I saw small woven blankets that decorated the living room walls. A number of both men and women often sat on aluminum lawn chairs under elm trees in the evenings. When teenage children were present, country western music played, usually from a parked car or truck. The men mostly wore blue jeans and western style shirts. Beaded western belts were common. Women wore shorts, housedresses, or jeans. The men over 40 years old wore conservative haircuts; younger men wore their long straight black hair tied in the back. Both the activity and the conversation seemed slow and deliberate. Everyone seemed at peace with the world and with each other.

The neighborhood bar sat on the corner of one major street and a side street like any in the area. The bar advertised with a nondescript name painted on an unlighted weathered board nailed above the door. Otherwise the building resembled the architecture of the area and could just as easily house a church or day-care center. The only descriptive markings were what appears to be territorial youth-gang graffiti on the back of the building out of sight to those driving by. Across from the bar sat another bar with a Hispanic name. On the third corner was another bar with no name, just a neon sign advertising beer. On the final corner stood a liquor store with bared windows, a light in the parking lot, and signs warning of the alarm system. Each visit I parked alone in the liquor store parking lot under the light and walked to the bar.

As I entered the building, the door stuck from the heat and humidity. I kicked it open; no one noticed. Music played from a jukebox in the center of the room that contained about fifteen barstools around a bar top covered with linoleum flooring. Restaurant-style booths scattered along two of the walls. A few tables with chairs sat on carpet that covered half of the floor. The carpet had been rolled out some time ago and pulsed with six inch high waves from repeated sweeping as people walked across it. The rest of the floor showed well-polished, well-stained concrete.

Everyone in the bar drank beer, about half from plastic pitchers and stained chipped plastic cups, about half from longneck bottles. Nothing was said, but everyone in the room noticed as I walked inside and sat down near the end of the bar. Shortly, the bartender walked over and I ordered a soft drink.

The Native American bartender looked like a beat-down laborer who had nowhere else to go. He wore casual, well-worn clothing and worked at a slow, constant, methodical pace without saying a word or providing eye contact to anyone. A small group sat at the other end of the bar. They consisted of Whites, Hispanics and Native Americans. Although diverse in their culture and appearance, they seemed almost like family in their interaction. They quietly talked about work, home, and life problems as easily as if they were at the kitchen table.

I sensed a questioning annoyance of my presence without anything empirical to support the feeling. Two pool tables sat on the polished concrete floor. About fifteen men and women played pool as casually as two old men play checkers in the city park. Quick and casual glances provided the only indication that I invaded someone s territory.

By midnight, I moved to a darker area still near the end of the bar. The crowd seemed to have forgotten my presence when two teenage boys entered the bar. The boys sat in the booth nearest the door that had been mysteriously left vacant the entire evening. The boys looked about fifteen years old and tried hard to act older and tougher than their age. They both wore oversize khaki shorts that hung down showing their underpants and the top portion of their buttock. They both wore oversize T-shirts that although soiled, looked as thought they had been pressed earlier in the day. They wore the same brand of British Knights tennis shoes. Finally, they both wore blue print bandanna style handkerchiefs folded and tied around their head with a square knot on their left temple.

As the boys walked in, one sat down at the booth and began to dig in his pocket. He removed a handful of wadded-up money that he threw on the table. Then he dropped his head down on the table as though to pass out or go to sleep. The second boy took the money, grabbed a used plastic beer pitcher from a nearby table and walked to the bar with an exaggerated yet non-descriptive gait. The bartender took the wadded-up money and filled the pitcher without washing the pitcher or looking at the boy.

Noticing me setting near the end of the bar, the boy walked over while he waited for the beer. He came just close enough to invade my personal space. He challenged me without saying a word. Two women left their male companions and began dancing to the music in front of the jukebox on the well-worn carpet. The bartender set the pitcher of beer on the bar with the boy s change. The pay phone rang and the bartender walked over to answer it. The boy picked up the change. He lifted his shirt with one hand while putting the money in his pocket with the other. He did this while never taking his eyes off me. As he lifted his shirt, I saw the unmistakable butt of a handgun protruding from his back pocket. As I saw the gun, I thought of the one-inch knife/nail-file that folds into one side of the money clip in my front pocket. My thought of bringing such a knife to a gunfight lightened the situation and brought a hidden grin. The boy returned to his table. I finished my RC Cola and left.

I became more accepted each time I returned to the neighborhood bar. I never developed the relationships that come from knowing someone since birth. I never looked like I had just worked a full day at the refinery. Although my differences were noticed, they were never questioned. People in the bar accepted the bar as part of their neighborhood, part of their culture. The single response when I asked how long the bar had been around was forever. Customers said that there was never any trouble inside the bar. Sometimes people took a fight or argument outside or if it was serious took it somewhere else.

Social controls emerged from the various subcultures in various areas of the room. Those in the small group at the end of the bar knew and interacted with the group playing pool. Then they returned to their group. Young boys, similarly dressed, coming into the bar always sat in the same booth near the door. They never again took notice of me. It was as if I, on repeated visits, had been granted my space in the dark, on a single stool near the other end of the bar.

Ponca City Restaurant Bar

I first visited the restaurant bar on a Friday night in late May. The 9:00 p.m. evening hung heavy with the hot, humid air from an afternoon that threatened yet never developed springtime thunderstorms. A reminder of an unseasonably warm winter lingered in the form of mosquitoes and buffalo gnats. The sky remained overcast both from storm clouds and from distant grass fires.

The bar resided on the main north-south drag through town. The area seemed clean, well trafficked and populated with small open-air strip malls, each containing less than a dozen small shops and stores. The parking lot seemed both dark and quiet. About half of the available parking spaces held cars. As I looked around, I could not easily identify the destination of the vehicle owners. For example, a parked car could just as easily patronized the family fun center next door as the restaurant itself.

As I walked inside the restaurant, there was no question that I entered a bar. A traditional bar covered a third of the north wall. Five tiers of liquor bottles with cork and chrome pouring spouts sat in front of a well-lighted backdrop mirror. Above the bar four 30-inch televisions in built-in cabinetry played without sound. Three TVs showed the same basketball game, the third played a rerun of the six o clock news. No one noticed. A canoe hung from one wall complete with paddles and fishing poles. The remainder of the walls held tennis rackets, baseball gloves, ski poles and all types of sporting equipment.

Fourteen wooden barstools lined the bar. The remainder of the bar contained four round tables with eight chairs each and 25 tables each with only two chairs. A polished brass rail separated the bar and bar stools from the remainder of the room.

As I walked into the bar, I found one person eating at the bar and people eating and drinking at three of the four large tables. Upon notice of my arrival, those at the large table in the back got up. One woman, the owner, greeted and directed me to a small table across from the bar. A second woman, a server, checked on other customers then took my order. A third woman walked toward the kitchen and the only man from the table stepped behind the bar. Piped in elevator-type music played continuously in the background.

Only one person sat at the bar. He wore a tan straw western hat, a long sleeve heavily starched western shirt, tight pressed blue jeans with sharp creases and cowboy boots. Clean cut describes this 30 year old recently shaven, shorthaired, well-scrubbed man who smelled of lite beer and Old Spice cologne. The man looked only at his food that in another setting could be called the blue-plate special. He paid for his meal without a ticket and got up to leave. As he walked away, the bartender called him by name saying see you tomorrow. The customer s gate, his unsteady stance, his blood shot eyes and his dilated pupils indicated a high degree of intoxication. He left without answering the bartender in the direction of a nearby motel. For the bartender, the encounter seemed well rehearsed and uneventful.

The second table contained a young man in his early 20s and two women of about the same age. Each seemed casually dressed as though they just stepped from a college classroom. They sat drinking frozen mixed drinks of various colors. The male drank three drinks as each of the women slowly smoked cigarettes, drank a single drink and chatted about the day s happenings. The male sat and drank without speaking.

The final table contained what at first seemed like an unusual group. The single man in his mid 30s drank one domestic beer. What appeared to be a three-year-old girl sat in an infant high chair between the man and the 30 year old woman to his right. Another woman about the same age sat to his left. Each person dressed casually. The women wore light cotton sleeveless blouses and either shorts or casual slacks. One woman wore flat shoes; the woman in shorts wore sandals without socks. Everyone at the table ate what looked and smelled like the pot roast or meat loaf special. The woman nearest the child asked for a box for leftovers.

Between the two women sat a younger woman in her late teens. This teen wore a short, black, moderately low-cut dress that seemed to cause her constant attention. Her black stockings and paten-urethane high-heeled shoes caused unsteady ankles from unfamiliarity. She seemed strangely out of place until conversation revealed her earlier graduation ceremony at the local high school. The bar owner later confirmed the graduation saying to me that the bar was wall-to-wall just an hour before I arrived. Those at the table received a telephone call from the bar phone, finished their meal and left after saying goodbye to the owner. This satisfied my questions about the people at the table; my questions about the owner s statements remained.

The casualness of the bar employees when I entered failed to support the owner s comments about a busy evening. The tables in the bar seemed orderly but lacked the look and smell of having been recently wiped clean. Each of the glasses at the bar appeared polished and in their place. Even the kitchen help, first seen at the table in the back, lacked purpose and urgency.

The owner later said that she opened the bar and two other bars in neighboring cities just seven months ago. She described business as great, mostly because of the good food. Appetizers ranged from chips and salsa at $2.59, to Buffalo wings, fried mushrooms and stuffed jalapenos at $6.99. Main courses ranged from kid s meal corny dogs at $1.99, to a $15.99 Porterhouse steak. The menu seemed complete within these ranges with the selections printed on photographs of sport figures and racecars.

Although the appearance and the availability of beer and liquor clearly labeled and licensed the restaurant as a bar, the attraction was food. On additional visits, I repeatedly heard the owner speak of just missing large crowds. I never saw over fifteen people in the bar. Some drank quietly alone or in small groups. Most had a drink or two with their meal and left. Formal social controls seemed unnecessary. People mostly came to eat and to sometimes drink with their meal and leave. Others drank with an agenda away from the restaurant and left. I left too; the restaurant closed each day at 10:00 p.m.

Ponca City Theme Bar

A family operated the Ponca theme bar. The bar opened in 1974 with a theme of the roaring 20s. Parts of the original theme waned over time; remnants remained. My first visit came in early June on a Friday night. I arrived shortly after 10:00 p.m. and found the bar closed. The following night, I arrived at 8:00 p.m. only to find that I needed a reservation. Determined, I finally made it in on my next attempt.

The bar was located in the rear of one of the City s larger outdoor strip shopping malls. To get to the bar, you must walk down an alley created by the rear of the mall buildings and the side of a detached movie theatre. The asphalt alley held trash dumpsters and loading docks for the respective buildings. It looked as though someone poured a new four-inch high sidewalk in the middle of the alley. The sidewalk ended at an open steel faced metal clad door. The area would have projected the fear of being mugged if it were not for the halogen lights that provide more light than the noontime sun.

I entered the bar by walking through the metal door into a small entryway where I met a locked wooden door. A small sign by the door read, Ring the bell. Pushing the buzzer caused a young girl to open a peephole in the door to ask if you had a reservation. With an affirmative reply, the door opened. In the 1970s, the hostesses wore flapper-style dresses and the cook, a double-breasted suit of the same era. At my visit, everyone dressed more casually. The decor remained obviously that of a 1920s speakeasy and supper club.

Downstairs in cramped quarters sat two tables with four chairs and two tables with two chairs. The bar was upstairs with eight barstools, surrounded by equally cramped tables and chairs. One upstairs wall contained a wine cellar where customers selected their own wine bottles from wooden racks. A gas grill occupied the center of the downstairs room. When the bar first opened, customers cooked their own meat. Cooking remained an option, however the meat during my research was most often cooked by the owner.

As the owner cooked, he visited with customers and braged that he only buys local beef and refrigerates the meat for fifteen days but never freezes it for better flavor. The bar accommodated 25 customers at tables and an additional five customers seated at the bar. Aside from the tables and chairs, the only furnishings included a small salad bar and a cash register near the door. No music played. The lack of music and the cramped quarters provided a sense of urgency to eat, drink and make room for someone else. The receptionist at the door enhanced this feeling by sometimes telling customers to enjoy their meal but their table is reserved for someone else in one hour.

Customers generally consisted of middle-aged couples and families. Most wore casual attire that reflected upper middle class. Occasionally a high school aged couple nervously dined as though on a first date and worrying about the bill. Generally, people came in family or business groups, ate and left. A table never sat idle over five minutes, just time to replace the white linen tablecloth. No one lingered outside. No one spent over 20 minutes at the bar without either leaving or being seated at a table.

A banquet room sat idle upstairs that seated another 25 people with room for a small band and dancing. The management still dressed in 1920s clothing for banquets and special events. In conclusion, the bar s theme changed.

The bar opened as a theme bar and returned to that theme for banquets and special events. The physical size, location and structure of the building supported a 1920s speak-easy theme. Because of the small size of the building, and only room for a bar on the upstairs level, the bar owner began emphasizing food. Emphasizing food, taking reservation and creating an atmosphere of hurry-up and make room for the next person eliminated many of the problems associated with drinking and intoxication. The transition also enhanced opportunity for profit. During three visits, not a single customer approached intoxication. The single bartender kept as busy as bartenders in other bars. He simply kept serving different customers.

I originally classified this bar based on the setting, history, style of operation and information provided by customers and advertisements. After visiting the bar and interviewing the owner and employees, I quickly reclassified the bar as sharing many more characteristics of restaurant bar than that of a theme bar.

Summary

With the appropriate data, I found each bar easy to classify as either a hotel bar, neighborhood bar, theme bar or restaurant bar. Even the Ponca City theme bar demonstrated a transition over time from one type to another, for cause. Each of the bars exhibited unique social controls dependent upon the type of bar and the culture of its setting. For example, the Ponca City hotel bar used many of the social control techniques observed at the Stillwater theme bar. This become explainable by advertising, cultural setting and clientele motivation.

The Ponca City hotel bar not only drew customers from the hotel, but from the community as well. This differed from the Stillwater hotel bar, which solely depended upon its hotel for revenue. The local franchise owner operated both the Stillwater hotel and the Ponca City hotel bars. The contractual arrangements and the Stillwater hotel bar residing fully within the hotel explained many differences between the Stillwater and Ponca City hotel bars. The Ponca City hotel bar advertising and soliciting patrons from throughout the community explained other differences. This influenced not only goals and motivations of the bar, but those social controls present within its culture.

In the hotel bar, patrons depended on the hotel for lodging, often in an unfamiliar community. Patrons also depended on the bar for their sole source of entertainment or to act out their individual agendas like meeting another person. If an individual was ejected from the hotel bar, they often had nowhere else to go but their room. This provided the bartender or manager a type of power and control not found in other settings. Outside the bar, parents, children and often highly visible security personnel provided social controls while customers entered and exited the bar. These social controls seemed to work well on the upper middle class clientele of the hotel bar.

Patrons depended on the neighborhood bar as an extended family. As such, other patrons as well as the bartender or manager shared the power and control which came from possible rejection of a patron. Although individual circumstances varied, patrons of the neighborhood bar sought something not found in the traditional family environment. This enhanced the patron s dependence on the neighborhood bar and further enhanced the power of the associated social controls. Often the patron expelled from the neighborhood bar was left with the hopeless-helpless feeling that they had no home away from the neighborhood bar.

I found social controls within the restaurant bar present but indistinguishable from other public business settings. Drinking and even social activities either surrounded or were secondary to eating. During time when business was brisk, the demand for tables forced customers to eat and leave. Further, the unfamiliarity of the person setting at the next table left little reason to stay.

Social controls within the theme bars also differed from social controls in other type bars. Both the agenda and culture of the theme bar supported a business environment and the bottom line. Theme bars sold beer, liquor, atmosphere, entertainment and for some, opportunity. From the management s perspective, when a customer interfered with the profit margin, swift and certain social controls in the form of bouncers and security personnel acted. There was no appeal. Customers in the bar usually possessed a well-defined, all-be-it personal, agenda. Sanctions for violating the rules of the bar held swift and certain ejection.

Outside the theme bar, social controls broke down. Individual emotions and intoxication rather than reason governed behavior. The infrequent police car driving by offered little social control with the windows up and the officer looking straight ahead.

These data showed a variety of social controls operate in bars. Data also showed that specific types of bars use the same social controls regardless of community laws concerning public drinking. For example, theme bars in Stillwater where public drinking is prohibited used the same social controls as theme bars in Ponca City where public drinking is allowed. I found the same trend with hotel, restaurant and neighborhood bars.

I also found that with the possible exception of the hotel bar, these social controls are not significantly reinforced and generalized when individuals leave the bar and continue to drink on public streets. Therefore, I concluded that differences in crime rates in cities before and after enacting public drinking prohibitions resulted from social controls in place on public streets and sidewalks. Many of these social controls are formal in the form of police. The collective behavior demonstrated in the street party ethnographies illustrated situations whereby the size of the crowd empowered individuals further diminishing social controls outside of bars and taverns. This conclusion failed to explain why some communities (and the same community at different times) exhibited different changes in rates of serious crime following public drinking bans.

NOTES

[1] This reference is a recreational guide written by a husband and wife. They recommend two cities in each state to visit based on a number of categories including a low crime rate. Stillwater entrepreneurs interpret this as meaning that Stillwater is one of the 100 safest cities in America, a claim not supported by other comparative measures.

[2] 1990 Federal Census population estimates are 38,268 for the City, 62,435, for the County, and 133,700 for a 30 mile radius of Stillwater.

[3] Multi-service listing is a cooperative listing among realtors, which lists all properties currently for sale. The list does not contain properties for sale by owner, nor properties exclusively listed by only one realtor. The list does provide a comparative value between communities.

[4] Streaking was a fad consisting of people running naked through public areas. Associated with flashing (wearing nothing except a long coat and periodically opening the coat to public view), the fad was nationwide and affected popular music and even the Academy Awards was once streaked. Both streaking and flashing were associated with this event.

[5] During this time, Oklahoma law permitted a female to drink alcoholic beverages at age 18, but required a male to be 21 years of age.

[6] Information is from a Report to the City Commission submitted to the Stillwater City Commission immediately following the event by then Stillwater Police Chief Hilary Driggs.

[7] The unpublished, undated report entitled Eskimo Joe s Weekend 1991 Visitation, Spending and Economic Impact was submitted by Lowell Caneday Ph.D., School of HPER, Oklahoma State University. In a follow-up letter dated January 18, 1993 to Stillwater City Manager Carl Weinaug, Caneday said that sales tax revenues would be a better measure of economic impact, however those records were not available for his study.

[8] Crowd estimates came from police press releases and newspaper reports. Police estimated the crowd by comparing the closely packed crowd to known area seating in the OSU football stadium.

[9] In 1987 the Downtown Merchants Association moved the Crazy Days celebration from it s traditional June date to a July date to correspond with anticipated traffic of the weekend street party event. Crazy Days is a weeklong celebration where merchants dress-up in crazy costumes and sell merchandise in the streets and sidewalks at a reduced price.

[10] The City Manager s request began with meetings between the Chief of Police and the District Attorney. Following these meetings, the District Attorney asked the City Manager by letter to end the street party because of the associated violence.

[11] Fearing an organized uprising from university students, the city commission refused to act on the drinking ordinance but placed the question to a vote of the people in a local election. The City spent over $2,000.00 to place this question on the ballet.

[12] Crime rates are defined as the number of reported crimes per 100,000 of a population.

[13] I also conducted a Tukey test on the same data. Tukey indicated statistical significance between during and after crime rates p=.022, but failed to show significance in the before and during rates p=.069.

Multiple Comparisons

Dependent Variable: CRIME
Tukey HSD

(I) TIME	(J) TIME	Mean Difference (I-J)	Std. Error	Sig.	95% Confidence Interval	
					Lower Bound	Upper Bound
1.00	2.00	5.6125	2.170	.069	-.4460	11.6710
	3.00	-1.5825	2.170	.753	-7.6410	4.4760
2.00	1.00	-5.6125	2.170	.069	-11.6710	.4460
	3.00	-7.1950*	2.170	.022	-13.2535	-1.1365
3.00	1.00	1.5825	2.170	.753	-4.4760	7.6410
	2.00	7.1950*	2.170	.022	1.1365	13.2535

*. The mean difference is significant at the .05 level.

[14] After subjectively reviewing the available data from the selected communities I decided to use comparisons of three years before and three years after enactment of their prohibition law for comparison. I based this decision on availability of data. For example, one community s crime statistics were reported by and included in the statistics for the county sheriff four years before enactment and could not be used. Two communities began reporting using the NIBRS rather than the UCR system four years after enactment and that data could not be used. Using three years before and three years after yielded the most reliable data while maintaining the largest sample for comparison.

[15] During this portion of research, I subjectively examined the arithmetic decrease in the before and after means. Later I conducted a one-way analysis of variance. The analysis of variance showed statistical difference in the original Stillwater drinking ban and in the Chico, California data.

[16] By non-participant observation, I mean that I did not consume alcohol while collecting these data.

[17] By average size for the community, I mean that the motel sits comfortably within its setting. An out-of-town visitor would not look at the motel and wonder what happens here to support a motel of this size or extravagance.

[18] This particular bar licensees the entire area inside the bar and outside throughout the enclosed courtyard for the purpose of consuming alcoholic beverages. This allows the bar to serve alcoholic beverages at events such as weddings and conventions without the necessity of obtaining a caterers licenses or a special events license for each event.

[19] Transporting an open drink or bottle of any type of alcoholic beverage in a motor vehicle constitutes a misdemeanor violation in Oklahoma. I took no action when witnessing these minor violations.

[20] This particular type of poker machine set to pay off for winning hands violated State gambling laws. Throughout each visit, no one took interest in the machine.

[21] Several years earlier the bar failed to renew it s State and local liquor license. These licenses cost more than the on-premise beer license. For this reason, the neighborhood bar only served beer and soft drinks.

[22] The status of a restaurant meant only that over 51% of the revenue came from the sale of something other than alcohol. Oklahoma State Law allows persons under 21 years of age to enter an establishment if their main purpose is something other than the sale of alcohol. From a cultural and social perspective, the business remained a bar catering to college students.

[23] Since it s founding this individual bar grew to a number of various theme bars and restaurants throughout the community. The bar employs 250 employees. At the time of my first visit, this particular bar employed a night manager, an assistant manager in charge of doormen/bouncers and an assistant manager in charge of bartenders.

[24] Ponca City demographic information courtesy a telephone interview with employees of the Ponca City Chamber of Commerce, September, 1997.

[25] The hotel in Stillwater maintained control over employees hired in the Stillwater hotel bar. The Stillwater contract also tied the control of the bar into the control of an adjacent restaurant with a local overseer hired by the motel.

CHAPTER 6

Data Analysis

In Chapter 5, I examined the before and during prohibition crime rates for Stillwater, OSU, Norman, and the State of Oklahoma. At that time, I accepted an $\alpha \leq .05$ as statistically significant. The difference between before Stillwater crime rates and during Stillwater crime rates is statistically significant at the .05 level. Likewise, a p-value greater than .05 indicates that the difference in before and during crime rates of OSU, Norman and the State of Oklahoma were not significant. I attributed the difference between Stillwater s and other crime rates to the existence of a public drinking ban.

I offered additional support by conducting an additional analysis of variance on the before, during and after Stillwater crime rates. These data also showed statistical significance ($p=.021$). The post hoc test indicates statistical difference between the before and during crime rates and statistical difference between the during and after crime rates. No statistical difference was indicated between the before the public drinking prohibition crime rates and the crime rates after the repeal of the public drinking law. This was expected. I initially attributed these results to the existence of a public drinking ban.

Later in Chapter 5, I identified nine additional cities with public drinking bans. Of these, seven showed mean decreases in crime rates following enacting public drinking laws. At the time I accepted these data to support my assumptions and hypothesis and continued to search for social controls inside and outside of various types of bars to account for these data.

The ethnographic studies showed similarities between not only Stillwater and Ponca City, but also between similar type bars in each community. If social controls remained constant in the same type bars where public drinking was both allowed and prohibited, could social controls on streets and sidewalks account for the decrease in serious crime when public drinking was banned? I reexamined the communities earlier identified with public drinking prohibitions. I reviewed their actual ordinance and performed an analysis of variance on their before and during enactment of their public drinking prohibitions.

Table 8
Analysis of Variance Table

Community	**F-Value**	**P-Value**
Stillwater 1978	6.914	.039
Stillwater 1994	3.413	.138
Ada	.768	.43
Manhattan	.964	.382
Boulder	.000	.988
Durant	.657	.463
Edmond	4.216	.109
Lawton	6.710	.061
Jenks	.2	.678
Lawrence	.909	.394
Chico	29.661	.002

Examining these data using the $p \leq .05$ standard of significance used in Chapter 5, I found significant differences in before and during crime rates in only the first Stillwater data and the data from Chico, California. Why was the Stillwater data different between the first ordinance and the second? What do Stillwater in 1978 and Chico have in common that are absent or diminished in the other communities and Stillwater in 1994? I began by contacting individual city governments.

I either telephoned and/or wrote each of the cities surveyed and inquired about their public drinking ordinance and its enforcement. I generally spoke with a court clerk, a police public information officer or a police crime analyst.

At Boulder I spoke with an employee in the Court Clerks office. I spoke with the Court Clerk in Jenks. Boulder officials did not remember their local ordinance and could not remember the last time it was enforced. The Jenks Court Clerk said, We were not computerized (at the time the ordinance was enacted) and therefore can only guess how many tickets were issued for the offenses in question. We write a lot of tickets now for minors in possession of beer and not any for consumption (in public). For the years 1985-1989 we probably averaged 3 to 5 tickets per month for possession —none for consumption. Boulder analysis of variance indicated a significance of p=.988, Jenks of p=.678. Therefore, a statistical difference in the means cannot be established.

I spoke with record clerks in the Ada and Manhattan police departments. Neither department kept computerized records to provide the rate or degree of enforcement. Each department knew of their ordinance and said that officers occasionally (but not very often) enforce the public drinking prohibition. Manhattan went on to say that their officers more often ask offenders (especially around Kansas State University) just to pour the beer out and do not even make a report. Ada analysis of variance indicated a significance of p=.43, Manhattan of p=.382. Ada represented one of two communities who did not indicate a mean decrease in serious crime following enactment of their public drinking prohibition.

I spoke with a public information officer with the Lawrence Police Department. Lawrence seldom enforced the ordinance. The ordinance was publicized and, used as a zoning issue so as not to create a downtown drinking area for students. The Durant Municipal Court Clerk said that the City of Durant did not computerize until November 1993, and, there is not a way to give you a fair or correct estimate of beer related charges during the time frame of 1982-1986. When questioned by telephone, she went on to say that the public consumption ordinance was not a well-known ordinance. I spoke with a crime analyst at the Edmond Police Department. Edmond said that their officers also do not make very many arrests, however, the exact number is unknown. Lawrence indicated an analysis of variance significance of p=.349, Durant of p=.463, and Edmond of p=.109. Durant represented the second of two communities surveyed that did not show a mean decrease in serious crime following enacting of their public drinking prohibition.

I telephoned a record supervisor at the Lawton Police Department. She said that computer records were not available and a hand search and count could not be performed. She did say that officers frequently used their public consumption ordinance. She referred to the ordinance as a useful tool and that officers wrote a lot of tickets for it (public consumption). Lawton indicated an analysis of variance significance of p=.061.

Finally, I contacted a clerk typist, an administrative technician, and finally the Chief of Police at the Chico Police Department. The Chico Police Chief said, It is a great tool. I don t have any idea how many, but we write the hell out of it and the noise ordinance too. It s the best tool that we have found against drunken riots. Chico indicated an analysis of variance significance of p=.002.

Each of the cities contacted could not provide exact data on the degree of enforcement of their public beer-drinking ordinance. Most cities cited a lack of computerization. Lawton said that officers write many tickets but could not provide an exact number. Lawton indicates a significance of p=.061. Chico said that they write the hell out of it. Chico indicates a significance of p=.002. Stillwater indicated a significance of p=.039 following the first enactment of the ordinance, but only a significance of p=.138 the first three years of Stillwater s second ordinance. All other communities indicated little or no enforcement and far from significant p-values.

Table 9
Enforcement of Public Drinking Bans

City	Action	Mean Difference	P-Values
Boulder	Unaware of law.	-.06	P=.988
Jenks	No enforcement	-3.88	P=.678
Ada	Infrequent enforcement	3.55	P=.43
Manhattan	Verbal warnings	-.11	P=.382
Lawrence	Publicizes ordinance	-3.14	P=.349
Durant	Not well known law	3.34	P=.436
Edmond	A few arrests	-4.37	P=.109
Lawton	A lot of tickets	-13.28	P=.061
Stillwater 1994	Decreasing verbal warnings	-4.44	P=.138
Stillwater 1978	Numerous arrests	3.21	P=.039
Chico	Write the hell out of it	-18.37	P=.002

P-values cannot be used as data to correlate crime rates with degrees of enforcement. However, information from telephone interviews suggests that such a relationship may occur. For further support of this hypothesis, I reexamined each of the Stillwater drinking prohibitions and compared Stillwater to the Chico public drinking prohibition.

Stillwater Crime Analysis

During the first Stillwater public drinking prohibition, police officers enforced the law by one of two methods. Officers either made a custodial arrest or issued a verbal warning and released the offender. A custodial arrest meant that officers searched and handcuffed the offender and sometimes impounded the offender s vehicle.[1] Officers then transported the offender to the police station where the suspect was either jailed or allowed to post a $100.00 bond. Records are unavailable of the number of verbal warnings issued during the life of the first ordinance. The following table indicates the number of custodial arrest made during the first Stillwater public drinking prohibition.

Table 10
Number of Arrests During
Stillwater s First Public Drinking Prohibition

Year	Number of Arrests
1978	109
1979	169
1980	69
1981	2

Data collected courtesy Stillwater Police College Intern Todd Parry.

These data show that Stillwater officers initially made a large number of arrests for the public drinking prohibition. The numbers of arrests then tended to decrease over time. These data generally corresponded to individual crime rates given in Table 6. The crime rate in 1978 was 23.09 with 109 arrests, all during the last six months of the year. The rate in 1979 was 24.88 with 169 arrests. The rate in 1980 was 24.37 with 69 arrests. And the rate in 1981 was 26.63 with two arrests. Generally, the more police make arrests for public drinking the lower the rate of serious crime.

To support this statement, a correlation became possible between the crime rate for a given year and the number of arrests made that year. I subjectively expected a negative correlation that would indicate that the more arrests made, the lower the crime rate.

Pearson correlation yields a correlation coefficient of $r = -.58$. I consider this a moderately high relationship especially considering that the ordinance was only enforced the last six months of the first year.

Table 11
Number of Public Drinking Arrest, Crime Rate Comparisons

Correlations

		ARRESTS	RATE
Pearson Correlation	ARRESTS	1.000	-.580
	RATE	-.580	1.000
Sig. (2-tailed)	ARRESTS	.	.420
	RATE	.420	.
N	ARRESTS	4	4
	RATE	4	4

Other information can be considered.

Several police procedures changed before Stillwater enacted its second public drinking prohibition. The second prohibition required police to issue either a verbal or a written warning before charging an individual with public consumption of beer. The fine remained at $100.00, but officers could then write a summons and release the offender at the scene. There were no longer custodial arrests, impounded vehicles and trips to police headquarters for either bond or jail unless officers charged the offender with another crime, such as disturbing the peace, at the same time.

During the entire first three years of the second ordinance, Stillwater officers issued four tickets per year for public consumption. Each of these twelve tickets accompanied a second more serious jailable charge, usually public drunkenness. The number of verbal warnings issued for violating the second Stillwater ordinance was available. This provided data for a comparison between the crime rates for a given year and the number of verbal warnings issued that same year. Again, for the data to be significant, I expected a negative correlation. This would indicate that the more verbal warnings that were issued, the lower the crime rate. The following table shows the number of verbal warnings issued for public consumption of beer since enactment of the second ordinance.

Table 12
Number of Warnings During
Stillwater s Second Public Drinking Prohibition

Year	Number of Warnings
1994	132
1995	146
1996	99
1997	30

A Pearson correlation yielded a correlation coefficient of r = .701. I considered this result spurious in that the decrease in number of warnings tended to correspond with general decreases in crime rates both on the local and national levels. In 1994, Stillwater crime rates totaled 45.33. In 1995 through 1997, the rates indicated 48.46, 45.70 and 44.75 respectively.

Overheard conversations of Stillwater officers indicated displeasure with the second ordinance. The officers working the bar districts were younger than those officers working the same assignment during the first law. Many of the younger officers frequented bars and drank during their off duty time. Some of these officers believed that the law was overly restrictive and should not be enforced. Other officers objected to a law that required a warning before either an arrest or a citation could be given. Older officers who believed in the effectiveness of the ordinance seldom enforced the new law fearing that public attitudes may again revoke the law. Regardless of the reason, the new law was neither strictly enforced nor carried as severe or as immediate a punishment as the first Stillwater law. The decrease in enforcement seemed to be tied most directly to these officer attitudes.

Table 13
Number of Warnings, Crime Rate Comparisons

Correlations

		RATE	WARNINGS
Pearson Correlation	RATE	1.000	.701
	WARNINGS	.701	1.000
Sig. (2-tailed)	RATE	.	.299
	WARNINGS	.299	.
N	RATE	4	4
	WARNINGS	4	4

Chico, California also showed statistically significant decreases in serious crime after enacting a local law prohibiting public consumption of beer.

Chico Crime Analysis

I began examining Chico's crime data by first examining the community and the events leading up to Chico enacting a local ordinance prohibiting public consumption of beer. The history of Chico generally focused on the historic development of the local college. In 1887, the school began with an eight-acre bequest by the town's founder. The campus known as the State Normal School opened two years later with 90 students and five faculty. In 1921, the school became Chico State Teachers College and in 1935, the school became Chico State College. In 1972, the name again changed to California State University, Chico. At the time of this study, the University supported 13,000 full-time students on a 119-acre main campus and 1,050 acres of farm and ranch land. The University provided both undergraduate and graduate programs with the most popular majors being elementary teaching, business administration and psychology. Ninety-eight percent of the student population came from California; 68 percent of the students were White. Hispanic (10%) represented the next highest ethnicity present. Sixty six percent of the faculty possessed doctorates or terminal degrees. The average student was between 24 and 25 years old.

The City of Chico lies 90 miles north of Sacramento, 174 miles northeast of San Francisco and two miles from the foothills of the Sierra Nevada Mountains. The Chico area seemed relatively rural with the population of Butte County at 12.6 persons per square mile compared to 196.3 persons per square mile for the entire State of California. Chico currently (1997) maintains a city population of 50,116 persons with a service area population of 92,500. The City occupies 26.95 square miles.

The population supported 64 churches, 25 hotels/motels/bed & breakfasts, two hospitals, and two shopping malls. The police department contained 74 sworn personnel and 43 civilian support personnel. The community contained 19,993 occupied single-family homes with an average of 2.38 persons per household. The average family income was $39,418 and the median age within the community was 24.6 compared to the average age of the community that was 31 years old. The City operated on an annual budget of $18.8 million dollars.

To understand the Chico, California ordinance, I examined video recordings of area TV news reports, newspaper clippings, video recordings of press conferences and video and minutes of City Commission meetings provided by the Chico Chief of Police.[2]

Events leading to the Chico public beer-drinking ordinance began in 1915 with an event sponsored by the local University. In 1915, Chico State University initiated an annual celebration called Pioneer Days. The event celebrated spring and the pioneer history and culture of the area. Over time, Pioneer Days became a community event supported by many local businesses. By 1973, students were using the event for drinking parties that often spilled into the streets. Police in 1973, responded to several hundred drunks with mounted officers who cordoned off city blocks to prevent looting. In 1987, the University canceled their sponsorship of the event after students began lighting bonfires in trash dumsters then rolled the burning dumsters into city streets.

The following year, 1988, local businesses resurrected the annual event. They formed a non-profit cooperation to support and promote Rancho Chico Days, a weeklong spring festival and celebration of local culture. The City promoted the event as good for local business and good for city-college relations. At the same time, the City Commission enacted a prohibition against public beer drinking and loud parties.

The first year of Rancho Chico Days included a parade with over 200 fraternity floats, a fair and a stage show with skits and costume presentations that supplemented other community events. A college fraternity built a small building for disadvantaged children. Toward the end of the week, the public began wearing pioneer costumes to the community events. Police heavily enforced both the public beer drinking prohibition and the loud party ordinances and increased the number of patrol officers working during the event. Things went well until 1990.

The Chico Chief of Police reported to the community on Thursday of the 1990 weeklong event that the community was quiet with few arrests and party related tickets. The first indication of trouble came at 10:01 p.m. Friday night when the host of a private party telephoned police and asked for help with an out-of-control party. Police responded with 20 officers in ten police cars. The officers wore helmets and carried riot batons. Officers reported 1,000 people drinking in the area and another 500 people drinking in a nearby street intersection.

Police ordered the crowd to leave the area by loudspeaker. The crowd responded by throwing rocks and beer bottles. Officers requested help from area communities and other law enforcement agencies. By 3:30 a.m., 40 officers quieted the crowd. One car burned in a bonfire in the street. Five officers received minor injuries. Police made 52 arrests, many for drunkenness-related offenses, but some for a felony charge of assault on a police officer.

Saturday night, 41 officers supplemented the six officers who usually patrolled the town. Another 45 uniformed officers sat at a command post in case of trouble. By 8:30, 30 officers escorted an airport fire truck to a bonfire burning a TV news vehicle. The fire also consumed residential wooden fences that were torn down and carried to the fire by the crowd. Another fire started near the police command post two blocks away and underneath high-voltage power-lines.

Following the incident, the Police Chief reported, Forty officers had to charge the crowd to save fifteen patrol cars and our command post. In all, 35 Chico officers, 138 officers from area law enforcement agencies, and 96 reserve officers made 42 arrests. Not included in the Chico data were 55 citations issued by State Alcoholic Beverage Control officers to liquor stores for selling beer to under age individuals.

Within the immediate area of the entire 1990 event, police made 109 arrests, many for assault on a police officer, a felony that carries a maximum five-year prison sentence.[3] An additional 116 party-related arrests occurred away from the area of what the police and media called riotous activity. During the celebration, eighteen Chico officers received minor injuries; 34 officers from area agencies received minor injuries; and 20 officers required hospitalization for cuts, contusions, and broken bones.

The City of Chico spent $18,500 for police overtime and $2,200 for vandalized street signs. The City estimated $7,000 damage to three fire trucks. Chico also spent $12,500 for medical treatment for injured police officers. Area law enforcement agencies that provided officers spent $30,000 for 1400 police person-hours.[4] Eventually, the City handled claims and expenses on an individual basis and did not publish a total cost to the City.

After the party, the City also received a claim for $2,300 for damage to a citizen s vehicle. The City received four complaints of brutality committed by Chico officers, four complaints of excessive force committed by unknown officers and one brutality complaint committed by an officer from an adjacent law enforcement agency. Only one complaint on an officer was investigated and turned over to the district attorney for criminal prosecution. The City Attorney later asked the City Commission for $40,000 for salary for an assistant City Attorney to help the District Attorney prosecute those arrested and charged during the celebration.

Summary

Stillwater and Chico both reacted to street party experiences by enacting local laws prohibiting the public consumption of beer. Both communities heavily enforced their ordinances when first enacted. The Chico law remained in force and the perceived need for enforcement of the ordinance became reinforced by the continued street parties and annual celebrations. With continued enforcement, the rate of serious crime significantly decreased.

In Stillwater, the first ordinance killed the associated street party. The party lacked the organized community support found in Chico. With the Stillwater party dying, the community and, based on the number of arrests, police officers lost interest in the beer drinking ban. Later Oklahoma State University students overturned the public drinking prohibition in a Stillwater City referendum election. In terms of enforcement, Stillwater officers enforced the drinking ban with custodial arrest, fines and impounded vehicles when first enacted. The rate of serious crime significantly decreased.

When Stillwater reenacted the public drinking prohibition, the law included a mandatory warning. Police procedure also changed that allowed officers to issue a ticket to violators. Custodial arrests and impounded vehicles no longer occurred unless there was another jailable offense. Officers made few arrests and after the first year and issued decreasing numbers of warnings. The second Stillwater public drinking prohibition failed to significantly impact serious crime.

These data suggest that the relationship between type and amount of police enforcement and degree of punishment of public drinking prohibitions and serious crime should be further explored.

NOTES

[1] Vehicles in which the driver is arrested and the vehicle is not legally parked or in which there is not a licensed driver to drive the vehicle are towed and impounded at the owners expense following a custodial arrest from the vehicle.

[2] Because Chico had experienced trouble in the past associated with Rancho Chico Days and because the Chief of Police had predicted no trouble in the future, area TV filmed events leading up the nights of the riots, interviews, and City Commission meetings following the event. The Chico Chief of Police made copies of these tapes available for this research.

[3] Chico averages 350 arrests per month.

[4] Under California law, mutual aid agreements require emergency service (including law enforcement) agencies to provide assistance to neighboring communities in times of emergencies. Host agencies are required to provide assistance without charge.

CHAPTER 7

Conclusion

This study began with a single observation. Two separate and distinct street parties and their associated crime and violence ended following passage of local laws that prohibit the public consumption of beer. After passage of the first public drinking prohibition, rates of serious crime significantly decreased. After four years of enforcement, citizens repealed the drinking prohibition and serious crime statistically increased to rates similar to those before enacting the prohibition. Rates of serious crime failed to decrease following passage of the second law despite both prohibitions and street parties took place in the same community at different times.

This study then identified ten communities that also passed local ordinances prohibiting the public consumption of beer. Eight of these communities experienced a decrease in serious crime rates after prohibiting the public consumption of beer. However, only one city (other than Stillwater) showed statistical significance at the $\alpha \leq .05$ level. Since a public consumption law does not prohibit beer drinking, only public drinking, I questioned what social controls were present inside bars that were diminished or absent when people drink on public streets and sidewalks. I questioned if identifying these social controls could account for changes in crime rates after passing public drinking prohibitions and why communities differed in their reaction to public drinking bans. I also questioned why Stillwater differed in its crime rate reactions to drinking prohibitions that were passed at different times.

To answer these questions, I established four categories of bars and studied the social controls at work inside and around these type bars both in Stillwater where public drinking is prohibited and in Ponca City where public drinking is allowed. The typology scheme worked well when given appropriate time for bar classifications. Non-participant observation provided the appropriate methodology for identifying social controls in operation. Finally, I found similar social controls operating inside similar type bars in both Stillwater and Ponca City. I conclude that if similar social controls operated inside bars both in communities that allowed and prohibited public drinking, then social controls operating outside bars might explain differences in rates of serious crimes after enacting public drinking prohibitions. I further conclude that my street party observations represent collective behavior with extreme loss of otherwise occurring social controls.

By surveying a number of communities with public drinking prohibitions, I found the degree of both enforcement and punishment varied. After further analysis of before and after crime rates, the data support several conclusions.

The data suggests that generally, the greater the enforcement and punishment, the greater the decrease in rates of serious crime. Further research into this relationship seems warranted. I found the swiftest and most certain social control inside bars. Formal and informal sanctions varied with the type of bar and the type of social control present.

Although the data are limited, the data also suggest that Chico is more successful in reducing serious crime by police writing tickets for their drinking prohibition than Stillwater (1978) where police made custodial arrests and impounded vehicles. Verbal warnings during the Stillwater second prohibition did not appear to make a significant impact on serious crime. Therefore, the punishment of a ticket and the associated fine appear to represent the most efficient enforcement to affect serious crime rates. Verbal warnings are not enough; arrest, jail and vehicle impoundment are too much.

To either write tickets or make custodial arrests, police must get out of their air-conditioned police cars and personally interact with potential offenders. Either the officer enforcing public drinking laws or the community police officer walking the bar beat provides immediate and certain presence of social control. Minor but significant punishment for violations completes the social control/deviance model.

This supports the findings of Smith and Gantin (1989) who found that 50 percent of people arrested on their first contact with police were never arrested again. This also supports Dewey s 1896 concept of the reflex arc and the cognitive process.

Dewey (1896) described this process as a patchwork of disjointed percept thought and behavior processes, not distinct, but operating as a single concrete whole continuously folding over each other in a process of coordination. I call this cognition. Specific to these observations, the process of being certainly and immediately punished for nuisance crimes, like public beer drinking, can be generalized as a deterrent from more serious violations.

One attribute of a good theory or model is external validity, generalizability or the ability to relate the theory to a wide range of social phenomenon. These data and the aspects of society that it examines relate well to community policing philosophies and the enforcement of nuisance laws.

Community policing techniques place police officers in close contact with citizens. Often working on foot, horseback or bicycle, community police officers work with citizens to establish needs of small business districts, parks and neighborhoods. This close contact provides both immediacy and a certainty when laws are violated. This close contact also establishes interpersonal relationships that allow less severe punishments for law violations. This occurs, for example, when Officer Finnegan, the local beat officer, catches Mrs. Henry s boy, Joey, stealing apples and puts the boy to work for George, the grocer, sweeping floors. Joey learns that if Officer Finnegan caught and punished him for stealing apples, think what would happen if Joey stole a car. Therefore, Joey does not steal cars, a cognitive process.

This same concept can be further generalized to enforcing nuisance laws such as junk vehicle ordinances, zoning requirements, begging, street performing and drinking beer on streets and sidewalks. The important aspect for generalization is the certainty, celerity and surety of real, but minor, punishment for violating social norms.

This study suggests that aggressively enforcing public drinking prohibitions with real but not burdensome punishment appears to decrease serious crime. Further research is needed when police records become more complete through computerization. Further research is also needed specifically looking at the enforcement of other nuisance laws beyond public drinking prohibitions. This study represents the beginning.

References

Accident Analysis and Prevention. (1997). Alcoholism at the time of injury among trauma center patients: Vehicular crash victims compared with other patients. Vol. 29, 6.

Amdur, L.H. (1963). *Copyright Law and Practice.* NY: Clark Boardman Co., Ltd.

Anderson, L.S., Chiricos, T.G., & Waldo, G.P. (1977). Formal and Informal Sanctions: A comparison of deterrent effects. *Social Problems,* 25, 103-114.

Antee, A. and Swinburn, J. (1990, January). Crowd management: an issue of safety, security, and liability. *Public Management,* 72(1), 16-19.

Adler, F., Mueller, G.O.W., Laufer, W.S. (1991). *Criminology.* NY: McGraw-Hill, Inc.

Bailey, W. (1976, July). Certainty of Arrest and Crime Rates for Major Felonies: A research note. *Journal of Research in Crime and Delinquency,* 145-154.

Ball, H.G. (1944). *The Law of Copyright and Literary Property.* Albany, NY: Banks and Co.

Bandura, A. (1986). *Social Foundations of Thought and Action: A social cognitive theory.* Englewood Cliffs, NJ: Prentice Hall.

Barnes, H.E. (1972). *The Story of Punishment: A record of man s inhumanity to man. 2d ed.* Montclair, NJ: Patterson Smith.

Beccaria, C. (1764). *On Crimes and Punishment.* Young, D. (Ed.). (1986). Indianapolis, IN: Hackett Publishing.

Bentham, J. (1789). *An Introduction to the Principles of Morals and Legislation.* Reprinted. Jacoby, J.E. (Ed.). (1979).

Classics of Criminology. Prospect Heights, IL: Waveland Press.

Berk, R.A. and Newton, P.J. (1985). Does arrest really deter wife battery? An effort to replicate the findings of the Minneapolis Spouse Abuse Experiment. *American Sociological Review*. 50, 253-262.

Berger, P.L. and Luckmann. (1966). *The Social Construction of Reality*. NY: Doubleday.

Bilchik, Shay. (1988, February). Combating Underage Drinking. *Office of Juvenile Justice and Delinquency Prevention Fact Sheet*. US Government Printing Office. Publication number FS-9875.

Black, H.C. (1979). *Black s Law Dictionary*. Fifth Ed. St. Paul, MN: West Publishing.

Chaiken, J.M., & Robinson, L. (1998, April). An analysis of National data on the prevalence of alcohol involvement in crime. Prepared for the Assistant Attorney General s National Symposium on Alcohol Abuse and Crime. Publication number NCJ-16832.

Chambliss W.J. & Seidman, R.B. (1971). *Law, Order, and Power*. Reding, MA: Addison-Wesley Publishing Co. .

Campbell, D.T. (1975). On the conflict between biological and social evolution and between psychology and moral tradition. *The American Psychologist*. 1103-26.

Chafetz, M.E. 1990, January). Managing alcohol in public facilities: caveat manager. *Public Management*. 72(1), 20-21.

Collins, J.J. (1977, Spring). Suggested explanatory frameworks to clarify the alcohol use/violence relationship. *Contemporary Drug Problems*. 15(1), 107-121.

Cook, P.J. (1980). Research in Criminal Deterrence: Laying the groundwork for the second decade. Morris, N. and Tonry, M.

(Ed.). *Crime and Justice: An annual review of research 2.* 211-268.

Cosper, R.L., Okraku, I.O., & Neumann, B. (1987). Tavern going in Canada: A national survey of regulars at public drinking establishments. *Journal of Studies on Alcohol.* 48(3), 252-259.

Denzin, N.K. (1989). *The Research Act.* Englewood Cliffs, NJ: Prentice Hall,.

Dewey, John. (1896). The Reflex Arc Concept in Psychology. *Psychological Review.* 3 357-370.

Durkheim, Emile. (1895). *The Rules of the Sociological Method.* Translation (1965) Solvay, S.A. & Mueller, J.H. NY: Free Press.

Eliott, D.S., Ageton, S.S. & Canter, R. J. (1979). An integrated theoretical perspective on delinquent behavior. *Journal of Research in Crime and Delinquency.* 16, 3-27.

Erickson, M.L. & Gibbs, J.B. (1998). Community Tolerance and Measures of Delinquency; Objective and perceptual properties of legal punishment and the deterrence doctrine. Center for the Study of Crime and Delinquency, National Institute of Mental Health. Grant MH22350. Washington, DC: US Government Printing Office.

Federal Bureau of Investigation. (1994). *Crime in the United States 1993 Uniform Crime Reports.* U.S. Department of Justice. Publication No. ISBN0-16-045321-6. Washington, DC: US Government Printing Office.

Fisher, R.A. (1949). *The Design of Experiments.* Edinburgh: Oliver and Boyd. .

Franke, D. and Franke, H. (1984). *Safe Places for the 80s.* Garden City, NY: Dial.

Gans, H. (1962). The West End: An urban village. in *The Research Act*. Golden, M.P. (Ed.). Itasca, IL: F.E. Peacock Publishers, Inc.

Geertz, C. (1983). Thick Description: Toward an interpretative theory of culture. In *Contemporary Field Research, A Collection of Readings,* by Emerson, R.M. (Ed.). Prospect Heights, IL: Waveland Press, Inc.

Gibbs, J.P. (1976). *Crime, Punishment, and Deterrence.* NY: Elsevier.

Glassner, B., Ksander, M., Berg, B. & Johnson, B.D. (1983). A Note on the Deterrent Effect of Juvenile verses Adult Jurisdiction. *Social Problems.* 31, 219-222.

Grasmick, H.G., and Green, D. (1980). Legal Punishment, Social Disapproval, and Internalization as Inhibitors of Illegal Behavior. *Journal of Criminal Law and Criminology,* 71, 325-335.

Grasmick, H.G. (1981). The Strategy of Deterrence Research: A reply to Greenberg. *Journal of Criminal Law and Criminology,* 72, 1102-1108.

Green, D.E. (1989a). Measures of Illegal Behavior in Individual-Level Deterrence Research. *Journal of Research in Crime and Delinquency,* 26, 253-275.

Green D.E. (1989b). Past Behavior as a Measure of Actual Future Behavior: An unresolved issue in perceptual deterrence research. *Journal of Criminal law and Criminology,* 80, 781-804.

Green, D.E. (1989c). The Effects of Sanction Threat on Self-Reported Drinking and Driving Behavior: A comparison of sampling procedures in perceptual deterrence research. *Free Inquiry in Creative Sociology,* 17, 165-173.

Greenberg, D.F. (1981). Methodological Issues in Survey Research on the Inhibition of Crime. *Journal of Criminal Law and Criminology,* 72, 1094-1101.

Hazlehurst, K.M. (1986). Alcohol, outstations and autonomy: an Australian Aboriginal perspective. *The Journal of Drug Issues.* 16(2). 209-220.

Harper, D.A. (1982). *Good Company.* Chicago, IL: University of Chicago Press. 139-145.

Hennessy, M. and Saltz, R.F. (1993, March). Modeling Social Influences on public drinking. *Journal of Studies on Alcohol,* 54(2), 139-145.

Homel, R., Tomsen, S., & Thommeny, J. (1992). Public drinking and violence: not just an alcohol problem. *The Journal of Drug Issues,* 22(3), 679-697.

Hirschi, T. (1969). *Causes of Delinquency.* Berkeley: University of California Press.

Holden, R.T. (1983). Rehabilitative Sanctions for Drunk Driving: An experimental evaluation. *Journal of Research in Crime and Delinquency,* 20, 55-72.

Jacoby, J.E. (1978). *Preventing Crime. The Deterrent Power of Prosecution.* Cramer, J.A. (Ed.). Beverly Hills, CA: Sage. 137-161.

Klepper, S., and Nagin, D. (1989). The Deterrent Effect of Perceived Certainty and Severity of Punishment Revised. *Criminology,* 27, 721-746.

Katzen, J., Cook, K., & Crouch, W. (1991). *Evaluating Information.* NY: McGraw Hill. 104-111.

Kotarba, J.A. (1984). One more for the road: The subversion of labeling within the tavern subculture. In *The Sociology of Deviance.* by Douglas, J.D. Boston: Allyn and Bacon Inc.

Krohn, M.D. & Massey, J.L. (1980, Autumn). Social control and delinquent behavior: An examination of the elements of the social bond. *The Sociological Quarterly.* 21. 529-544.

Lamson, R.L., Crowther, C., Spacy, B., & Crump, V. (1968). *Crime and Penalties in California, Part Two.* Prepared for the Assembly Office of Research for the Assembly Committee on Criminal Procedure. California Legislature Assembly Rules Committee. Sacramento, CA.

Lanza-Kaduce L. & Bishop, D.M. (1986). Legal Fictions and Criminology: The jurisprudence of drunk driving. *Journal of Criminal Law and Criminology,* 77, 358-378.

Lieberman, E. (1994, Spring). The Rational Deterrent Theory Debate: Is the dependent variable elusive. *Security Studies,* 3, 384-427.

Lieberman, E. (1995, Summer). What makes Deterrence Work? Lessons from the Egyptian-Israeli Enduring Rivalry. *Security Studies,* 4, 833-892.

Lieberman, E. (1995, October). Deterrence Theory: Success or failure in Arab-Israeli Wars? McNair Paper Number 45. Chicago: Institute for National Strategic Studies, National Defense. University.

Lyons, W. (1984, July). Deterrent Theory and Punishment of the Innocent. *Ethics,* 4, 346-348.

Maestro, M.T. (1973). *Cesar Beccaria and the Origins of Penal Reform.* Philadelphia: Temple University Press.

Maguire, K. & Pastore, A.L. (Ed.). (1994). *Sourcebook of Criminal Justice Statistics. 1993.* U.S. Department of Justice, Bureau of Justice Statistics, Publication No. NCJ-148211. Washington, DC: US Government Printing Office.

Maynard, E. and Gibbs, J. (1978, February). Objective and Perceptual Properties of Legal Punishment and the Deterrence Doctrine. *Social Problems,* 25, 253-264.

McCaghy, C. (1985). *Deviant Behavior: Crime, Conflict, and interest groups. Second edition.* NY: Macmillan.

Mead, G.H. (1934). *Mind, Self, and Society; From the standpoint of a social behaviorist.* Chicago: University of Chicago Press.

Meier, R. & Johnson, W. (1977, April). Deterrence as Social Control: The legal and extralegal production of conformity. *American Sociological Review,* 42, 292-304.

Miller, D. (1968). *Public Knowledge of Criminal Penalties: A research report.* Sacramento, California Assembly on Criminal Procedure. San Francisco, CA: Social Psychiatry Research Associates.

Miller, D. (1968). *Deterrent Effects of Criminal Sanctions.* Sacramento, CA: Assembly on Criminal Procedure.

Minor, W.W. & Harry J. (1892). Deterrent and Experimental Effects in Perceptual Deterrence Research: A replication and extension. *Journal of Research in Crime and Delinquency,* 19, 190-203.

Murdoch, D., Pihl, R.O., & Ross, D. 1990. Alcohol and crimes of violence: present issues. *The National Journal of the Addictions,* 25(9), 1065-1081.

National Center for Policy Analysis. (1996). *Does Punishment Matter?* Dallas, TX: http://www.public-policy.org/~ncpa/ba/ba101.html.

National Criminal Justice Association. (1997, November). Local Law Enforcement Slow to Implement NIBRS, Says search study. *Justice Bulletin*, 17, 11. 1. Washington, DC: US Government Printing Office.

National Criminal Justice Association. (1998, April). Alcohol Involved In 40 Percent of Violent Crimes and Fatal Accidents According to Justice Department. *Justice Bulletin*, 18. 4, 11. Washington DC: US Government Printing Office.

North American History — 1700-1800. (2000). [On-line]. Available: http://www.wfu.edu/Academic-departments/History/whistory/timeline/namerica/17-18.htm.

O Neal, Glenn. (1998, March 30). Colleges run bars to battle binges. *USA Today.* 4-d.

Parsons, T. & Bales, R. B. (Ed.). (1955). *Family, Socialization, and Interaction Process*. NY: Free Press.

Paternoster, R., Saltzman, L.E., Chiticos, T.G. & Waldo, G.P. (1982). Perceived Risk and Deterrence: Methodological artifacts in perceptual deterrence research. *Journal of Criminal Law and Criminology,* 73, 1238-1258.

Paternoster, R., Saltzman, L.E., Waldo, G.P. & Chiricos, T.G. (1983a). Estimating Perceptual Stability and Deterrent Effects: The role of perceived legal punishment in the inhabitation of criminal involvement. *Journal of Criminal Law and Criminology,* 74, 270-297.

Paternoster, R., Saltzman, L.E., Waldo, G.P. & Chiricos, T.G. (1983b). Perceived Risk and Social Control: Do sanctions really deter? *Law and Society Review,* 17, 457-479.

Pfohl, Stephen. (1994). *Images of Deviance and Social Control; A sociological history*. NY: McGraw-Hill, Inc.

Piliavin, I., Gartner, R., Thornton, C. & Matsueda, R.L. (1986). Crime, Deterrence, and Rational Choice. *American Sociological Review*, 51, 101-119.

Reckless, W.C. (1973). *The Crime Problem.* 5th ed. NY: Appleton-Century-Crofts.

Reckless, W.C. & Dinitz, S. (1972). *The Prevention of Juvenile Delinquency: An Experiment.* Columbus: Ohio State University Press.

Ross, L.H. (1984). *Deterring the Drinking Driver.* Lexington, MA: D.C. Healt and Company. .

Ross, L.H. (1981-82). Deterrence of Drinking and Driving in France: An evaluation of the law of July 12, 1978. *Law and Society Review*, 16, 345-374.

Saltzman, L., Paternoster, R., Waldo, G.P. & Chiricos, T.G. (1982). Deterrent and Experimental Effects: The problem of causal order in perceptual deterrence research. *Journal of Research in Crime and Delinquency*, 19, 172-189.

Sampson, R.J. & Laub, J.H. (1990, October). Crime and deviance over the life course: the salience of adult social bonds. *American Sociological Review,* 55, 609-627.

Sandhu, H. (1977). *Juvenile Delinquency: Causes, control, and prevention*. NY: Lexington, MA McGraw-Hill.

Schiraldi, V. and Godfrey, M. (1995, April). *Homicides Up After Executions: How have homicide rates been affected by the death penalty in California*. San Francisco, CA: Center on Juvenile and Criminal Justice.

Schiraldi, V. and Godfrey, M. (1995). *How Have Homicide Rates Been Affected by the Death Penalty in California*? Berkeley, CA: Center on Juvenile and Criminal Justice.

Sellin, T. (1967). *Capital Punishment*. NY:. Harper & Row.

Shapiro, P. & Votey, JR. H.L. (1984). Deterrence and Subjective Probabilities of Arrest: Modeling individual decisions to drink and drive in Sweden. *Law and Society Review*, 18, 583-604.

Silberman, M. (1976). Toward a Theory of Criminal Deterrence. *American Sociological Review,* 41, 442-461.

Smith, D.A. & Gartin, P.R. (1989). Specifying Specific Deterrence: The influence of arrest on future criminal activity. *American Sociological Review,* 54, 94-105.

Smith, H.W. (1991). *Strategies of Social Research*. St. Louis: University of Missouri Press. 148.

Spartacus Encyclopedia. (2000). British History 1700-1900. [On-line]. Available: http://www.spartacus.schoolnet.co.uk/parlimentA.hym.

Stitt, B.G., & Giacopassi, D.J. (1992, Autumn). Alcohol availability and alcohol-related crime. *Criminal Justice Review,* 17(2). 268-279.

Sutherland, E.H. (1940). White collar criminality. *American Sociological Review,* 5, 1-20.

Temple, Linda. (1998, March 30). Drinking in tradition. *USA Today*. p. 1-d.

Thio, A. (1988). *Deviant Behavior.* New York: Harper Collins Publishers, Inc. 48.

Thrasher, R.R. (1995, July). Managing the annual street party. *FBI Law Enforcement Bulletin,* 64, 7.

Tittle, C.R. and Rowe, A.R. (1974. Certainty of Arrest and Crime Rates: A further test of the deterrence hypothesis. *Social Forces,* 52, 455-462.

Trager, J. (1996). *The People s Chronology.* Henry Holt and Company.

US Department of Education. (1993). Youth and Alcohol; Selected reports to the Surgeon General. Washington DC: US Government Printing Office. US 1993 333-019/80040.

US Department of Justice. (1984). *Uniform Crime Reporting Handbook.* Washington DC: US Government Printing Office. Publication No. 0-445-197.

US Department of Justice, Office of Justice Programs, Bureau of Justice Statistics. September, (1988). Survey of youth in custody; Bureau of Justice Statistics special report. Washington DC: US Government Printing Office.

Washbrook, R.A.H. (1977). Alcoholism versus crime in Birmingham, England, *International Journal of Offender Therapy and Comparative Criminology,* 21 (2), 166-173.

Watts, Alan. (1957). *Introduction to Zen Buddhism.* Mt. Tremper, N.Y: Dharma Communications.

Wellford, C.R. (1974, August). Crime and the Police; A multivariate analysis. *Criminology,* 12.2, 195-213

Wiatrowski, M.D., Griswald, D.B. & Roberts, M.K. (1981). Social control theory and delinquency. *American Sociological Review,* 46, 525-541.

Williams, F.P. and McShane, M.D. (1994). *Criminological Theory.* Englewood Cliffs, New Jersey: Prentice-Hall. 182.

Williams, K.R. & Hawkins, R. (1986). Perceptual Research on General Deterrence: A critical review. *Law and Society Review,* 20, 545-571.

Wilson, O.W. & McLaren, R.C. (1977). *Police Administration.* NY: McGraw-Hill.

Yoder, S. (1978, Spring). Criminal Sanctions for Corporate Illegality. *Journal of Criminal Law and Criminology,* 69, 44.

APPENDIX A

Local Ordinances

Stillwater, OK Public Beer Consumption Ordinance (Adopted 4-5-94)

Sec. 3-92. Consumption of non-intoxicating alcoholic beverages in public places; warnings permitted; exceptions allowed; penalty.

(a) No person, whether minor or of age, shall consume or possess with intent to consume, or possess an open container of, non-intoxicating alcoholic beverages or beer upon any street, alley, roadway or sidewalk in the city, or in or upon any property owned by or under the control or the city, excepted as authorized herein.

(b) Notwithstanding the provisions of subsection (a) of this section, the consumption or possession of non-intoxicating alcoholic beverages by persons twenty-one (21) years of age or older on land owned or under the control of the city is permitted at:

(1) The Stillwater Municipal Airport as may be designated by written policies of the airport authority board with the approval of the mayor and city commission.

(2) The Stillwater Community Center as may be designated by written policies of the Stillwater Community Center Board with the approval of the mayor and city commission.

(3) Lakeside Golf Course as may be agreed under the terms of the lease agreement.

(c) Before issuing a citation for a violation of this section, any police officer of the city may give an oral warning, or issue a written warning ticket. If the person or persons receiving the oral warning or warning ticket do not discontinue the violation, a citation for ordinance violation shall be issued. If it appears necessary to make an arrest to preserve the public peace, a police officer may make an arrest for a violation of this section, with or without a previous oral warning or warning ticket.

(d) Any person violating the provisions of this section shall be guilty, upon conviction, of a misdemeanor and punished by a fine not to exceed one hundred dollars ($100.00) or by appropriate community service not to exceed twenty (20) hours. (Ord. No. 2472, / 2, 4-5-94)

Ada, OK Public Beer Consumption Ordinance Number 1515 (Adopted 10-20-1980)

AN ORDINANCE AMENDING SECTION 4-10 OF THE CODE OF ORDINANCES OF THE CITY OF ADA, OKLAHOMA, PROHIBITING THE DRINKING, CONSUMPTION, OR POSSESSION OF INTOXICATING AND NON-INTOXICATING BEVERAGES IN PUBLIC: AND DECLARING AN EMERGENCY.

BE IT ORDAINED BY THE COUNCIL OF THE CITY OF ADA, OKLAHOMA:

That section 4-10 of the Code of Ordinances of the City of Ada, Oklahoma, is hereby amended to read as follows:

SECTION 1.

(a) It shall be unlawful for any person who is drunk or in a state of intoxication to appear or be upon or in any street, alley, place of business or other public place, or for any person to drink or consume any intoxicating or non-intoxicating liquor or beverage upon or in any street, alley, place of business or other public place within the city.

(b) It shall be unlawful for any person to knowingly possess any intoxicating or non-intoxicating liquor or beverage upon or in any street, alley, place of business or other public place except in the original container which shall not have been opened and the seal upon which shall not have been broken and from which the original cap or cork shall not have been removed; provided that, this subsection shall not apply to licensed private clubs or to retail dealers licensed to sell non-intoxicating beverages for consumption on the premises.

(c) As used therein the term non-intoxicating beverage shall have the same meaning provided in Section 4-89 of the Code of Ordinances of the City of Ada, Oklahoma.

SECTION 2.

EMERGENCY CLAUSE. It being immediately necessary for the preservation of the public peace, health and safety, an emergency is hereby declared to exist, by reason whereof this ordinance shall take effect and be in full force from and after its passage and approval.

Velma, OK Public Beer Consumption Ordinance (Adopted July 1993)

ORDINANCE NO. 1993-3
AN ORDINANCE OF THE TOWNSHIP OF VELMA, OKLAHOMA, AMENDING SECTION 10-401 TO AMEND PUBLIC INTOXICATION AND DRINKING PROHIBITED, AND DECLARING AN EMERGENCY.

WHEREAS, the Town of Velma desires to add the words: It is unlawful for any person to drink intoxicating liquor or non-intoxicating beverage upon or in any street, alley, or other public place or in any public building within the town. It is unlawful to use, sell, or furnish to another any illegal drug or narcotic in any place in the town except as legally prescribed by a physician.

EMERGENCY, WHEREAS, It being immediately necessary for the preservation of the peace, health, safety and welfare of the Town of Velma, Oklahoma, and the inhabitants thereof that the provisions of the ordinance be put into full force and effect, an emergency is hereby declared to exist by reason whereof the ordinance shall take effect and be in full force from and after passage as provided by law.

Manhattan, KS Public Beer Consumption Ordinance (Adopted 11-3-87)

MANHATTAN CODE: Sec 4-2. Consumption in certain places forbidden.

(a) It shall be unlawful for any person to drink or consume alcoholic liquor or cereal malt beverage, or to have in possession an open container holding such cereal malt beverage or alcoholic liquor, while upon the public streets, sidewalks, alleys, parting lots, roads, or highways within the city, or upon property owned by the state or any governmental subdivision thereof, or inside vehicles while upon the public streets, sidewalks, alleys, parting lots, roads or highways within the city.

(b) Neither subsection (a) nor K.S.A. 41-719 shall apply to persons consuming or possessing alcoholic liquor or cereal malt beverage within Sunset Zoological Park, if the person is participating in a function sponsored by The Sunset Zoological Park & Wildlife Conservation Trust or the Friends of Sunset Zoo, and the function is for the purpose of promoting or improving Sunset Zoo. The function shall be approved, in advance, by the city manager, and shall be at a time when it does not interfere with other zoo activities or the public s use of the zoo. Prior to the commencement of such function, the city manager shall issue a permit, designating the date of such function, the hours during which such function shall be conducted, and the location within Sunset Zoo where such function will be conducted. No person shall possess or consume alcoholic liquor or cereal malt beverage within Sunset Zoological Park except as set forth on the permit issued by the city manager. The person in charge of such function shall have such permit present and available at the function, and shall present it to any law enforcement officer requesting same. The exemption set forth in this subsection shall not apply to any function until said permit has been issued.

Boulder, CO Public Beer Consumption Ordinance Ordinance No. 5003 (Adopted 1986)

TITLE 5 GENERAL OFFENSES
Chapter 7 Alcohol Offenses

5-7-2 **Possession and Consumption of Alcoholic Beverages in Public Prohibited.**

(a) No person within the city limits shall possess an opened container of or consume any malt, vinous, or spirituous liquor or fermented malt beverage in public, except upon premises licensed for consumption of the liquor or beverage involved.

(b) For purposes of this section opened container means any container other than an original closed container as sealed or closed for sale to the public by the manufacturer or bottle of the liquor or beverage. If an original container has been unsealed, undone, or opened in any manner, it is an opened container for purposes of this section.

(c) For purposes of this section in public means:

   (1) In or upon any public highway, street, alley, walk, parking lot, building, park, or other public property or place, whether in a vehicle or not:

   (2) In or upon those portions of any private property upon which the public has an express or implied license to enter or remain or;

   (3) In or upon any other private property without the express or implied permission of the owner or person in possession and control of such property or such person s agent.

(d) The following property owned or managed by the city is excluded from the coverage of this section during the hours of 8 a.m. to 11 p.m.: Coot Lake, Boulder Reservoir, Flatirons Golf Course, East Mapleton Ball Fields, and Stazio Recreation Complex, but if a special event permit for the sale of liquor or fermented malt beverage has been issued for all or a portion of such property pursuant to Section 12-48-101, et seq., C.R.S., then no person shall take or consume any malt, vinous, or spirituous liquor or fermented malt beverage onto or in the area designated in such permit except in accordance with such permit if a sign has been posted giving notice of the time and location of the area so restricted.

(e) It is an affirmative defense to a charge of violating this section that the premises were licensed by the city or by the State of Colorado for the consumption of the liquor or beverage involved, and any judge shall take judicial notice of the official records of such license and dismiss forthwith any charge to which this defense applies. If such dismissal is ex parte, the judge shall notify the city attorney, who may petition the court for permission to re-file the charge.

(f) It is a specific defense to a charge of violating this section that:

(1) The owner of the property involved or the owner s agent gave express permission to the accused or to members of the accused or to members of the accused s class to perform the acts complained of or;

(2) Accused was transporting the liquor or beverage from one place where it could be lawfully consumed directly and without delay to another such place, and the container was at all times during the transportation capped, corked, or otherwise re-closed with a firmly affixed waterproof lid. When the liquor or beverage was being transported in a motor vehicle, this defense is only available if the container was in the trunk or was not otherwise immediately accessible to the driver or any passenger

(g) No person shall drive or sit in the driver s seat of any motor vehicle, other than one carrying passengers for hire, in which a violation of subsection (a) of this section is occurring.

Moore, OK Public Beer Consumption Ordinance (Adopted July 20, 1992)

Section 3-212. Consumption of Non-Intoxicating Alcoholic Beverages in Public Places; Penalty; Exception.

A. No person, whether minor or of age, shall consume or possess with intent to consume, non-intoxicating beverages or beer in any public place, or upon any public street.

B. Any person violating the provisions of this section shall, upon conviction, be guilty of a misdemeanor and shall be punished as provided in Section 1-108 of this Code, or by appropriate community service not to exceed (20) hours.

C. The provisions of this section shall not prohibit a person who is of age from consuming such beverages in any place licensed to dispense beer as provided for in 37 Okla. Stat. / 163.11.

Section 2. **Severability**. If any of the provisions of this ordinance are determined to be unconstitutional or unlawful by any court of competent jurisdiction, the remainder shall be several and unaffected.

Section 3. **Repealer**. Any ordinance or parts thereof in conflict with this section are hereby repealed.

Section 4. **Emergency**. It being immediately necessary for the preservation of the public health, peace, safety and welfare, and emergency is hereby declared to exist by reason of which this ordinance shall become effective upon its passage and publication as provided by law.

Durant, OK Public Beer Consumption Ordinance (Adopted 6-2-81)

<u>SECTION 3-207 POSSESSION IN PUBLIC</u>

A. It is unlawful for any minor to be in possession of any non-intoxicating alcoholic beverage or beer while such person is upon any public street, road, or highway, or in any public building or place.

B. It is unlawful for any person to possess or have in his control an opened container of non-intoxicating beverage while such person is upon any public street, highway, alley, thoroughfare, right-of-way, sidewalk, public park or grounds, or upon, about or within any public building or public parking lot within the city. Possession of an opened container of non-intoxicating beverage is allowed only within any duly licensed tavern, club or retail dealer which is legally permitted to sell such non-intoxicating beverage for on-premises consumption.

<u>SECTION 3-208 DRINKING IN PUBLIC</u>

It is unlawful for any person, whether a minor or of age, to drink any non-intoxicating beverage while such person is upon any public street, alley, or other public highway, or in any public building or other public place, within the city. This section shall not prohibit a person who is of age from drinking such beverage in a place licensed to sell it for consumption on the premises.

Edmond, OK Public Beer Consumption Ordinance (Adopted 1984 Revised 1985)

8.08.300 Prohibition against carryout of open containers.

(a) It shall be unlawful and an offense for any person, owner, operator, manager or employee to permit or allow any patron or person to exit the premises of any establishment licensed by the ABLE Commission or any establishment where non-intoxicating beverages containing more than one-half of one (1/2 of 1%) percent alcohol by weight are sold for consumption on the premises with an open container of intoxicating beverage or non-intoxicating beverage as defined herein.

(b) It shall be unlawful and an offense for any person to take from any establishment licensed by the ABLE Commission or establishment where non-intoxicating beverages are sold for consumption on the premise an open container of intoxicating beverage or non-intoxicating beverage as defined herein.

(c) Exemption. Provided, however, this ordinance shall not be applicable to retail liquor containers which are carried from the promises by patrons. This exemption shall not be applicable to transporting open retail liquor containers in vehicles.

(d) Penalty. Any person who shall violate the provisions of Subsections (a) or (b) shall be deemed guilty of an offense against the City and upon conviction thereof shall be punished by fine and costs not to exceed One Hundred Dollars ($100.00).

Sapulpa, OK Public Beer Consumption Ordinance Ordinance No. 1234, // 1,2. (Adopted 1967)

Sec. 3-35. Consumption and transportation on streets, etc.

It shall be unlawful to drink non-intoxicating beverages as defined in this section while upon the streets and public ways of the city, including drinking of such beverages while in a vehicle on public streets and ways.

It shall be unlawful to transport in a vehicle, or by any other means, non-intoxicating beverages as herein defined upon the streets and ways of the city in a container which has been opened or the original cap or seal of which has been removed or broken, or which has no cap or seal; provided, that this section shall not apply if such beverages are transported in the trunk rear compartment or outside compartment of a vehicle and not accessible to the occupants of such vehicle.

Lawton, OK Public Beer Consumption Ordinance (Adopted 4-26-88 Revised 9-14-93)

SECTION 4-211 CONSUMPTION OR POSSESSION OF NON-INTOXICATING BEVERAGES IN PUBLIC PLACES; PROHIBITED; EXCEPTION.

A. It shall be unlawful for any person to consume or possess non-intoxicating beverages on land owned or under the control of the City, except as hereinafter provided.

B. Notwithstanding the provisions of Subsection A of this section, the consumption or possession of non-intoxicating beverages on land owned or under the control of the City is permitted at:

    1. Lake Lawtonka, Lake Ellsworth, municipal golf course, and the municipal airport restaurant.
    2. On and within the vicinity of Shepler Park, the Lawton Public Library Plaza, Great Plains Museum, McMahon Auditorium, and Lawton Community Theater during organized cultural, artistic, national or international events sponsored by a charitable organization, as that term is defined in Section 4-290- of this Code, or by the City of Lawton.

Jenks, OK Public Beer Consumption Ordinance (Adopted 1981 Revised 4-1984)

/2-3-4. Public consumption and intoxication prohibited.

No person within the City shall drink non-intoxicating alcoholic beverages on any public property, nor shall any person be intoxicated on any public property within this city.

Lawrence, KS Public Beer Consumption Ordinance
Ordinance Number 5114
(Adopted 1981)

4-215. CONSUMPTION AND POSSESSION PROHIBITED IN PUBLIC.

No person shall drink, consume or possess an open container of cereal malt beverage upon public streets, alleys, sidewalks, roads, highways, or public parking lots; or inside vehicles while upon public streets, alleys sidewalks, roads, highways, or public parking lots; or at the Lawrence Municipal Pool, Community Building, south Park Center, East Lawrence Center, Holcom Sports Complex, Lyon Street Ball park, Hobbs Ballpark, Woody Ballpark and Broken Arrow Ballpark; or on any private property without the consent of the owner.

Chico, CA Public Beer Consumption Ordinance Ordinance Number 1728 (Adopted April 14, 1988)

Chapter 9.30

POSSESSION AND CONSUMPTION OF ALCOHOLIC BEVERAGES

Sections:
9.30.010 Purpose.
9.30.020 Definitions.
9.30.030 Prohibition on the consumption of alcoholic beverages.
9.30.050 Signage required in retail establishments engaged in the packaged sale of alcoholic beverages.
9.30.060 Signage prohibiting the consumption of alcoholic beverages in parking lots on property containing two or more residential dwelling units.

9.30.010 Purpose.

This chapter is adopted pursuant to the municipal affairs provisions of Section 201 of the City Charter for the purpose of regulating the possession and consumption of alcoholic beverages upon certain public and private properties. (Ord 1728 (part))

9.30.020 Definitions.

Unless the contrary is stated or clearly appears from the context, the following definitions shall govern the construction of the words and phrases used in this chapter:

A. Alcoholic Beverage. The term alcoholic beverage means alcohol, spirits, liquor, wine, beer, and every liquid or solid containing alcohol, spirits, liquor, wine, or beer, and which contains one-half of one percent or more of alcohol by volume and which is fit for beverage purposes either alone or when diluted, mixed, or combined with other substances.

B. Consumption of Alcoholic Beverages. The phrase consumption of alcoholic beverages and/or the phrase consume an alcoholic beverage means the drinking or other ingestion of an alcoholic beverage.

C. Open Container of Alcoholic Beverages. The phrase open container of alcoholic beverages means a bottle, can, or other receptacle which contains alcoholic beverages and has been opened, or a seal broken, or the contents partially removed.

(Ord. 1728 (part))

9.30.030 Prohibition on the consumption of alcoholic beverages.

It shall be unlawful for any person to consume an alcoholic beverage upon any of the following properties within the city:

A. Upon any public street, sidewalk, alley, parking lot, or other property which is owned by or leased to the city and open to members of the general public, except for:
   1. Any city park or playground in which the possession and consumption of alcoholic beverages Is regulated by the park rules adopted in Title 12R of this code;
   2. Any portion of the Chico Municipal Airport in which the possession and consumption of alcoholic beverages is regulated by the airport rules and regulations adopted in Title 11R of this code;
   3. Any city property which is leased to a third party in which the lease agreement does not prohibit the possession and consumption of alcoholic beverages; and
   4. Any portion of a public street, sidewalk, alley, parking lot or other property owned by or leased to the city in which the sale of alcoholic beverages is permitted as part of a franchise granted by the city council pursuant to Chapter 14.60 of this code; and

B. Upon any private parking lot which is located on property used for commercial purposes, except where the owner or other person entitled to the possession of the parking lot has given his or her prior consent to the consumption of alcoholic beverages within such private parking lot; and

C. Upon any private parking lot which is located on property containing two or more residential dwelling units where such parking lot is posted with a sign prohibiting the consumption of alcoholic beverages in a manner hereinafter provided for by this chapter.

(Ord. 1728 (part), Ord. 1877/1, Ord. 1887, Ord. 1911/1, Ord. 2056)

9.30.060 Signage prohibiting the consumption of alcoholic beverages in parking lots on property containing two or more residential dwelling units.

The owner of property containing two or more dwelling units may prohibit the consumption of alcoholic beverages within any parking lot on such property by posting a sign in plain view at or near each driveway and pedestrian entrance to the parking lot which sets forth such prohibition substantially in the following form: It is unlawful for any person to consume an alcoholic beverage in this parking lot. Violations are punishable by a fine of up to $500.00. Chapter 9.30 of the Chico Municipal code. Such sign shall be not less than seventeen inches by twenty-two inches in size, shall contain lettering at least one inch in height, and shall be mounted so that the lower edge of the sign has a minimum height of four feet above ground level and the maximum height of the sign does not exceed seven feet above ground level.

(Ord. 1877/4, Ord. 1911/2)

Oklahoma State Statutes
Alcoholic Beverages on Public School Property

Definition: Defining the term public school. The term public school as used in these rules and regulations, shall include all schools supported, in whole or in part, by taxation of any kind or character within the State of Oklahoma, and shall also include all schools which may be attended by the public offering educational instruction equivalent to that offered in public grade schools, public high schools, public preparatory schools, and colleges and universities having authority to award recognized degrees.[a]

Pupils-Searches: The superintendent, principal, teacher, or security personnel of any public school in the State of Oklahoma, upon reasonable suspicion, shall have the authority to detain and search or authorize the search, or any pupil or property in the possession of the pupil when said pupil is on any school premises, or while in transit under the authority of the school, or while attending any function sponsored or authorized by the school, for dangerous weapons, controlled dangerous substances, as defined in the Uniform Controlled Dangerous Substance Act, intoxicating beverages, non-intoxicating beverages, as defined by Section 163.2 of Title 37 of the Oklahoma Statutes, electronic paging devices or for missing or stolen property if said property be reasonably suspected to have been taken from a pupil, a school employee or the school during school activities. The search shall be conducted by a person of the same sex as the person being searched and shall be witnessed by at least one other authorized person, said person to be of the same sex if practicable.[b]

---

[a] Article 2, Section 13, Rules and Regulations of the Alcoholic Beverage Laws Enforcement Commission, State of Oklahoma, Revised September 1987.

[b] Title 70, Section 24-102, paragraph 1, Oklahoma State Statutes, 1971.

Alcoholic Beverages and Other Drugs — As set forth in local, state and federal laws, and the rules and regulations of the University, Oklahoma State University prohibits the unlawful possession, use, or distribution of illicit drugs and alcohol by students and employees in buildings, facilities, grounds, or other property owned and/or controlled by the University or as part of University activities.

Under OSU regulations, no 3.2 beer or other alcoholic beverage is allowed in OSU housing, including fraternities and sororities, except for married student housing, regardless of age. Furthermore, under the same regulations, the possession/consumption of 3.2 beer or alcohol by those of legal age (over 21) is allowed only in certain designated, non-public places on the OSU campus, properties and facilities . [c]

---

[c] Oklahoma State University Catalogue and Handbook, 1998.

APPENDIX B

Crime Statistics and Analysis

Stillwater, OK Crime Statistics and Analysis Before and After Public Beer Drinking Prohibition

Stillwater 1991								
Before								
Population	Crime Rate	Murder	Rape	Robbery	Assault	Burglary	Larceny	Auto Theft
37018	45.95	1	18	18	54	432	1125	53
37449	42.91	1	9	10	68	354	1111	54
36730	41.3	2	16	15	68	294	1080	42
*37065.6	*43.3867	*1.33333	*14.3333	*14.3333	*63.33333	*360	*1105.33	*49.6667
After								
37037	45.33	0	7	19	75	315	1217	46
37744	48.46	0	9	14	91	351	1314	50
38008	45.7	0	17	19	98	352	1190	61
*37596.3	*46.4967	*0	*11	*17.3333	*88	*339.333	*1240.33	*52.3333

*Represents average value of preceding set

ANOVA

		Sum of Squares	df	Mean Square	F	Sig.
CRIME	Between Groups	14.508	1	14.508	3.413	.138
	Within Groups	17.003	4	4.251		
	Total	31.511	5			

Ada, OK Crime Statistics and Analysis Before and After Public Beer Drinking Prohibition

Ada								
Before								
Population	Crime Rate	Murder	Rape	Robbery	Assault	Burglary	Larceny	Auto Theft
17509	38.04	1	0	0	7	120	507	31
15787	37.44	4	3	5	12	82	445	40
15591	43.1	1	2	5	8	115	477	64
*16295.6	*39.5266	*2	*1.66666	*3.33333	*9	*105.666	*476.333	*45
After								
15929	35.53	1	6	5	15	143	367	29
16443	45.86	0	4	2	28	213	472	35
16862	48.75	1	2	11	15	216	526	51
*16411.3	*43.38	*0.66666	*4	*6	*19.33333	*190.666	*455	*38.3333

*Represents average value of preceding set

ANOVA

		Sum of Squares	df	Mean Square	F	Sig.
ADA	Between Groups	22.272	1	22.272	.768	.430
	Within Groups	115.943	4	28.986		
	Total	138.215	5			

Manhattan, KS Crime Statistics and Analysis Before and After Public Beer Drinking Prohibition

Manhattan								
Before								
Population	Crime Rate	Murder	Rape	Robbery	Assault	Burglary	Larceny	Auto Theft
32686	47.11	0	9	7	52	265	1164	43
33964	49.35	0	2	11	70	275	1265	53
32235	52.27	0	7	12	81	217	1331	37
*32961.6	*49.5766	*0	*6	*10	*67.6666	*252.333	*1253.33	*44.3333
After								
33161	50.78	0	12	7	75	202	1331	57
37712	48	0	13	8	76	204	1464	45
37976	49.64	2	12	16	88	311	1417	39

*Represents average value of preceding set

ANOVA

		Sum of Squares	df	Mean Square	F	Sig.
Manhattan	Between Groups	395.119	1	395.119	.964	.382
	Within Groups	640.176	4	410.044		
	Total	035.295	5			

Boulder, CO Crime Statistics and Analysis Before and After Public Beer Drinking Prohibition

Boulder								
Before								
Population	Crime Rate	Murder	Rape	Robbery	Assault	Burglary	Larceny	Auto Theft
81056	70.43	0	20	49	175	1130	4028	307
82413	71.13	2	17	50	170	1170	4139	314
79875	80.95	0	23	56	134	1272	4663	318
*81115	*74.17	*.67	*20	*51.67	*159.67	*1190.67	*4276.67	*313
After								
77166	72.52	1	13	46	124	931	4217	264
77191	71.26	1	15	31	135	866	4190	263
76358	78.54	0	14	35	120	879	4719	233
*76905	*74.11	*.67	*14	*37.33	*126.33	*892	*4375.33	*253.33

*Represents average value of preceding set

ANOVA

		Sum of Squares	df	Mean Square	F	Sig.
CRIME	Between Groups	6.0E-03	1	6.0E-03	.000	.988
	Within Groups	99.473	4	24.868		
	Total	99.479	5			

Durant, OK Crime Statistics and Analysis Before and After Public Beer Drinking Prohibition

Durant								
Before								
Population	Crime Rate	Murder	Rape	Robbery	Assault	Burglary	Larceny	Auto Theft
11005	52.07	2	0	9	23	124	370	45
11904	65.94	3	4	5	24	133	554	62
12288	63.07	0	1	6	34	134	539	61
*11732.3	*60.36	*1.66666	*1.66666	*6.66666	*27	*130.333	*487.666	*56
After								
12601	55.79	2	1	12	38	165	434	51
13080	62.46	1	1	6	53	175	533	48
12612	72.87	0	0	7	68	206	575	63
*12764.3	*63.706	*1	*0.66666	*8.33333	*53	*182	*514	*54

*Represents average value of preceding set

ANOVA

		Sum of Squares	df	Mean Square	F	Sig.
DURANT	Between Groups	33.041	1	33.041	.657	.463
	Within Groups	201.209	4	50.302		
	Total	234.251	5			

Edmond, OK Crime Statistics and Analysis Before and After Public Beer Drinking Prohibition

Edmond								
Before								
Population	Crime Rate	Murder	Rape	Robbery	Assault	Burglary	Larceny	Auto Theft
37888	48.22	2	9	20	128	229	996	113
41038	44.08	3	9	19	43	621	1000	114
41075	45.53	5	3	15	12	580	1131	124
*40000.3	*45.943	*3.33333	*7	*18	*61	*476.666	*1042.33	*117
After								
46261	45.07	15	8	15	34	587	1257	169
50462	39.93	0	12	33	29	528	1265	148
50232	39.7	0	12	15	39	539	1246	143
*48985	*41.566	*5	*10.6666	*21	*34	*551.333	*1256	*153.333

*Represents average value of preceding set

ANOVA

		Sum of Squares	df	Mean Square	F	Sig.
EDMONI	Between Groups	28.733	1	28.733	4.216	.109
	Within Groups	27.263	4	6.816		
	Total	55.995	5			

Lawton, OK Crime Statistics and Analysis Before and After Public Beer Drinking Prohibition

Lawton								
Before								
Population	Crime Rate	Murder	Rape	Robbery	Assault	Burglary	Larceny	Auto Theft
85812	68.92	5	56	188	380	1654	3280	351
81988	79.43	6	57	150	385	1986	3612	316
81707	74.53	7	51	110	346	1977	3306	293
*83169	*74.2933	*6	*54.6666	*149.333	*370.333	*1872.33	*3399.33	*320
After								
83188	56.46	3	42	120	411	1356	2527	238
80561	57.31	4	69	91	492	1252	2483	226
81314	69.26	9	55	118	605	1360	3209	276
*81687.6	*61.01	*5.33333	*55.3333	*109.666	*502.666	*1322.66	*2739.66	*246.666

*Represents average value of preceding set

ANOVA

		Sum of Squares	df	Mean Square	F	Sig.
LAWTON	Between Groups	264.670	1	264.670	6.710	.061
	Within Groups	157.769	4	39.442		
	Total	422.439	5			

Jenks, OK Crime Statistics and Analysis Before and After Public Beer Drinking Prohibition

Jenks								
Before								
Population	Crime Rate	Murder	Rape	Robbery	Assault	Burglary	Larceny	Auto Theft
5125	29.46	0	1	0	5	43	92	10
5836	24.85	0	0	1	0	57	82	5
6024	26.23	0	1	2	0	51	94	10
*5661.66	*26.8466	*0	*0.66666	*1	*1.66666	*50.3333	*89.3333	*8.33333
After								
6178	20.72	0	0	1	0	37	84	6
6413	26.51	1	0	0	0	73	84	12
6506	21.67	0	1	3	1	40	84	12
*6365.66	*22.9666	*0.33333	*0.33333	*1.33333	*0.33333	*50	*84	*10

*Represents average value of preceding set

ANOVA

		Sum of Squares	df	Mean Square	F	Sig.
JENKS	Between Groups	25.462	1	25.462	.200	.678
	Within Groups	510.321	4	127.580		
	Total	535.782	5			

Lawrence, KS Crime Statistics and Analysis Before and After Public Beer Drinking Prohibition

Lawrence								
Before								
Population	Crime Rate	Murder	Rape	Robbery	Assault	Burglary	Larceny	Auto Theft
52524	64.92	1	18	43	170	809	2180	189
52003	66.02	1	20	56	140	782	2232	202
52582	71.7	1	18	45	129	991	2397	189
*52369.6	*67.5466	*1	*18.6666	*48	*146.333	*860.666	*2269.66	*193.333
After								
53178	66.89	2	17	41	121	872	2354	150
53553	67.17	3	17	52	144	792	2389	200
54840	58.35	1	14	41	139	702	2149	154
*53857	*64.1366	*2	*16	*44.6666	*134.666	*788.666	*2297.33	*168

*Represents average value of preceding set

ANOVA

		Sum of Squares	df	Mean Square	F	Sig.
LAWRENC	Between Groups	17.442	1	17.442	.909	.394
	Within Groups	76.748	4	19.187		
	Total	94.190	5			

Chico, CA Crime Statistics and Analysis Before and After Public Beer Drinking Prohibition

Chico								
Before								
Population	Crime Rate	Murder	Rape	Robbery	Assault	Burglary	Larceny	Auto Theft
30830	109.34	1	27	36	255	648	2226	178
33506	87.27	2	22	35	124	640	1914	187
33736	102.65	1	17	27	116	594	2388	320
*32690.6	*99.753	*1.33333	*22	*32.6666	*165	*627.333	*2176	*228.333
After								
35926	93.19	2	20	29	104	636	2282	275
40079	76.75	3	40	39	152	610	2005	227
40913	74.21	2	39	39	82	672	1973	256
*38972.6	*81.383	*2.33333	*33	*35.6666	*112.666	*639.333	*2086.66	*252.666

*Represents average value of preceding set

ANOVA

		Sum of Squares	df	Mean Square	F	Sig.
CRIME	Between Groups	613.853	2	806.926	29.661	.002
	Within Groups	473.163	5	94.633		
	Total	087.015	7			

Oklahoma State University Crime Statistics and Analysis Before and After Stillwater Public Beer Drinking Prohibition

OSU								
Before								
Population	Crime Rate	Murder	Rape	Robbery	Assault	Burglary	Larceny	Auto Theft
18000	14.33	0	0	0	2	54	253	3
19476	17.05	0	3	1	1	68	254	5
21000	16.71	0	3	1	2	84	258	3
*19492	*16.03	*0	*2	*0.66666	*1.66666	*68.6666	*255	*3.66666
After								
18200	13.96	0	1	1	4	66	1331	1
18500	13.89	0	1	0	6	53	1464	2
19125	14.27	1	0	1	0	67	1417	7
*18608.3	*14.04	*0.33333	*0.66666	*0.66666	*3.33333	*62	*1404	*3.33333

*Represents average value of preceding set

ANOVA

		Sum of Squares	df	Mean Square	F	Sig.
CRIME	Between Groups	5.940	1	5.940	5.310	.083
	Within Groups	4.475	4	1.119		
	Total	10.415	5			

Index

Ada. 5, 68, 106, 107, 109, 137, 138, 158
Adler 7, 123
Ageton 125
alcohol consumption 1, 2, 3, 4, 12
Amdur 45, 123
analysis of variance 44, 45, 64, 65, 67, 103, 105-108
Anderson 26
arrests. 1, 26, 51, 56, 107, 109, 110, 111, 115-118, 120
assumptions 12, 33, 105
attachment 10, 11, 16
Bailey 27
Bandura 29
bar classifications 48
Barnes 85
Beccaria 16, 20, 21, 22-24, 27
belief systems 17
Bentham 23, 24, 27
Berg 25
Berger 15
Berk 27
Bilchik 1
binge drinking 1
BJS 8
Black 2, 9, 85
Boulder .. 5, 68, 106, 109, 142, 160
California State University 113
Campbell 15
case study 4, 5, 12, 42
celerity . 16, 23, 24, 34, 35, 36, 37, 41, 121
certainty 16, 23, 24, 26, 27, 34, 35, 36, 37, 41, 121
Chaiken 2
Chico 5, 44, 68, 103, 106, 108, 109, 113-118, 120, 151, 152, 153, 166
Chiricos 26
classical conditioning 28
classical school 20, 24
cognition 4, 11, 28, 29, 34, 35, 36, 37, 39, 121
college bars 10
commitment 16
community policing 33, 49, 121
comparisons 41, 111, 113
conclusion 13, 29, 97, 100
conditioned response ... 11, 39
containment theory 18, 19
context 6
Cook 25
correlation 1, 3, 17, 25, 27, 110, 111, 112
crime ... 1-9, 12, 14, 16, 20, 22-25, 27, 29, 31, 33, 36-39, 41-46, 49, 50, 51, 53, 55, 62-64, 66-68, 100-103, 105-107, 109-113, 117, 119-121, 124, 133, 134
crime rate 7, 23, 25, 34, 41, 43, 45, 49, 62-67, 105, 110-113, 119, 120, 123, 133, 156, 158-167
criminal behavior 34
curtilage 9, 47
death 11, 21, 22, 24, 132
definition of terms 7, 48
demonology 20

Denzin 49
deterrence 4, 12, 16, 20, 23-25, 27, 29, 36-38, 41, 49, 52, 125, 127, 130, 131, 133
deterrence doctrine.... 20, 129
deterrent 22, 23, 24, 26, 27, 29, 36, 37, 121, 123
Dewey 28, 29, 121
Dinitz 19
domestic violence....... 1, 3, 27
drunkenness 3, 33, 77, 111, 115
Durant 5, 68, 106, 107, 109, 145, 161
Durkheim 15, 21
Edmond.. 5, 68, 106, 107, 109, 146, 162
enforcement...... 41, 109, 130, 133, 154
Erickson 25
Ethical considerations 48
ethnic bars 10
ethnographic.... 41, 43, 44, 49, 52, 105
ethnography.................. 55, 85
external validity.......... 49, 121
FBI 7, 8, 46, 133
fear 11, 23
Federal Bureau of Investigation 7, 8, 46, 53, 63
Franke 55
gang.................. 59, 61, 84, 90
Gans 44
Gantin......................... 26, 120
Gartner 25
gay bars 10
Geertz........................... 12, 45
generalizability................ 121
Gibbs 24, 25, 27
Glassner 25
Godfrey........................ 25, 27
Green 26
Harper 6, 31
Hirschi 16, 17, 20, 29, 35
Hobbs.................. 15, 31, 150
home .. 1, 3, 10, 11, 35, 59, 62, 69, 72, 75-78, 86, 91, 99
Homel 2
hotel . 9, 10, 43, 47, 48, 68, 69, 73, 86, 87, 88, 98, 100, 104
hotel bar 86
hypothesis 12, 24, 38, 41, 105, 109
ideal-type 43, 68
index crimes....... 7, 33, 34, 51
inner containment 18
internal validity 50
involvement 17
Jacoby 27
Jenks 5, 68, 106, 109, 149, 164
Johnson 25, 27
Katzer 49
Klepper 25
Kotarba 44
Krohn 29
Ksander 25
Lamson 25
Lawrence 5, 68, 106, 107, 109, 150, 165
Lawton ... 5, 68, 106, 107, 108, 109, 148, 163
Lieberman 25
Luckmann 15
Maguire................................ 1
Manhattan 5, 68, 106, 107, 109, 140, 159
Marx 21
Matsueda............................ 25

McLaren............................27
McShane............................15
Mead............................15
Meier............................25, 27
methodology 4, 12, 25, 43, 44, 49, 50, 119
Miller............................25, 27
Minor............................34, 120
model............................23, 33, 34
Moore............................5, 144
Morgan............................50
motel............................*See* hotel
murder............................7, 8, 27, 75
Murdoch............................1
Nagin............................25
neighborhood bar...10, 11, 43, 48, 74, 77, 89, 90, 92, 98, 99, 104
Newton............................27
NIBRS............8, 44, 103, 130
non-participant observation..5, 12, 14, 41, 43, 45, 47, 49, 50, 68, 103
Norman............................62, 64, 105
nuisance laws3, 33, 36, 38, 49, 121
O'Neal............................1
Oklahoma State University ..6, 50, 55-57, 59, 61-64, 69, 80, 86, 101, 105, 117, 155, 167
outer containment............................18
Parsons............................15
participant observation..... 119
Pastore............................1
Paternoster............................25, 26
Pfohl............................22, 23, 31
Pihl............................1
Piliavin............................25
pioneer days............................114
Ponca City.... 5, 43, 44, 45, 47, 51, 68, 85, 86, 89, 93, 96, 98, 99, 105, 119
positivist school............................20
post hoc............................66, 105
predictions............................37
public drinking. 3, 5, 9, 12, 35, 41-47, 49, 50, 57, 61-68, 84, 99, 100, 105-107, 109-112, 117, 119-121, 125, 127
public drinking bans........ 109
pull factors............................19
punishment... 4, 11, 15, 16, 20, 21, 22, 23, 24, 26, 27, 29, 34, 36, 37, 39, 41, 51, 112, 117, 120, 121, 125, 131
push factors............................18
P-values............................109
Rancho Chico............................118
rape............................7, 8, 25
rates of death............................2
rational thought 28, 29, 36, 39, 49
rationale............................35
recidivism............................25, 29
reckless 16, 18, 19, 20, 29, 35, 131
reflex arc............................28, 121
reliability............................49, 50
restaurant bar9, 10, 43, 77, 79, 93, 98, 99
Robinson............................2
Ross............................1
Rowe............................25, 27
sales tax............................61
Saltzman............................26
Sandhu............................18
Sapulpa............................5
Schirald............................27

Schiraldi 25
Sellin 27
serious crime 3, 4, 7, 30, 38, 41, 42, 49, 64, 68, 100, 107, 110, 119, 120
severity. 16, 23, 24, 26, 27, 34, 36, 37, 41
Silberman 25
singles bars 10
Smith 26, 120
social bonds 16, 17, 35
social control ...4, 9, 12, 15-18, 20, 28, 29, 31, 33-35, 37, 38, 41, 49, 98, 99, 120
social setting 21, 37
sports bars 10
statistical difference 103, 105, 107
Stillwater ...5, 6, 42, 43-45, 47, 48, 51, 55-57, 59, 61-69, 74, 77, 80, 85-88, 98, 99, 101, 103-106, 108, 109, 110-112, 117, 119, 120, 135, 136, 156, 167
Stillwater Hotel Bar 69
Stillwater neighborhood bar 74
Stillwater restaurant bar 77
Stillwater theme bar 80
Stitt 1
streaking 14, 101
street party4, 5, 12, 42, 44, 58, 61, 100, 102, 117, 120, 133
strip bars 10
survey 45, 127, 133
tax 9, 59, 61, 101
Temple 1, 129
theme bar9, 43, 48, 80, 83, 84, 89, 96-99
thick description 12, 43, 45
Thio 29
Thommeny 2
Thornton 25
tickets27, 53, 67, 69, 107, 108, 109, 111, 115, 120
Tittle 25, 27
Tomsen 3
two-way analysis of variance67
Uniform Crime Report.... 7, 8, 44, 46, 62, 103
validity 49
Velma 5
victim 1, 3, 75
violence...... 3, 35, 44, 57, 102, 119, 125, 127, 130
violent crime 1, 7
Voltaire 22
Waldo 26
warnings.................. 112, 113
Washbrook 1
Watts 28
Wellford 25
Wiatrowski 29
Williams 15
Wilson 27